PSYCHOLOGICAL COUNSELING RESEARCH FOCUS

**WITHDRAWN
UTSA LIBRARIES**

UTSA DT LIBRARY RENEWALS 458-2440
DATE DUE

PSYCHOLOGICAL COUNSELING RESEARCH FOCUS

JAMES A. PATTERSON
AND
IRINA N. LIPSCHITZ
EDITORS

Nova Science Publishers, Inc.
New York

Copyright © 2008 by Nova Science Publishers, Inc.

All rights reserved. No part of this book may be reproduced, stored in a retrieval system or transmitted in any form or by any means: electronic, electrostatic, magnetic, tape, mechanical photocopying, recording or otherwise without the written permission of the Publisher.

For permission to use material from this book please contact us:
Telephone 631-231-7269; Fax 631-231-8175
Web Site: http://www.novapublishers.com

NOTICE TO THE READER

The Publisher has taken reasonable care in the preparation of this book, but makes no expressed or implied warranty of any kind and assumes no responsibility for any errors or omissions. No liability is assumed for incidental or consequential damages in connection with or arising out of information contained in this book. The Publisher shall not be liable for any special, consequential, or exemplary damages resulting, in whole or in part, from the readers' use of, or reliance upon, this material.

Independent verification should be sought for any data, advice or recommendations contained in this book. In addition, no responsibility is assumed by the publisher for any injury and/or damage to persons or property arising from any methods, products, instructions, ideas or otherwise contained in this publication.

This publication is designed to provide accurate and authoritative information with regard to the subject matter covered herein. It is sold with the clear understanding that the Publisher is not engaged in rendering legal or any other professional services. If legal or any other expert assistance is required, the services of a competent person should be sought. FROM A DECLARATION OF PARTICIPANTS JOINTLY ADOPTED BY A COMMITTEE OF THE AMERICAN BAR ASSOCIATION AND A COMMITTEE OF PUBLISHERS.

LIBRARY OF CONGRESS CATALOGING-IN-PUBLICATION DATA

Psychological counseling research focus / James A. Patterson and Irina N. Lipschitz (editors).
    p. cm.
 Includes bibliographical references.
 ISBN 978-1-60456-041-1 (hardcover)
1. Counseling psychology--Research. I. Patterson, James A. II. Lipschitz, Irina N.
BF636.6.P79 2007
158'.3--dc22
                              2007043489

Library
University of Texas
at San Antonio

Published by Nova Science Publishers, Inc. ✤ *New York*

CONTENTS

Preface		vii
Chapter 1	Prevention Programs for Relationship Distress and Violence: Importance, Exemplars, and Strategies for Recruitment *Tara L. Cornelius, Kieran T. Sullivan and Ryan C. Shorey*	1
Chapter 2	The Effects of a Psycho-Educational Group Intervention on the Quality of Life of Young Women with Breast Cancer *Joan R. Bloom, Susan L. Stewart, Carol D'Onofrio, Judith Luce, Priscilla Banks, Pat Fobair and Merrilee Morrow*	23
Chapter 3	A Model of Educational Video Intervention for Preventive Care in the Emergency Department *Yvette Calderon, Ethan Cowan and Marianne Haughey*	47
Chapter 4	Graduate Counseling Students Success Counseling Undergraduate Students as Clients: A Model for Training *Maureen C. Kenny*	59
Chapter 5	Social Stories as a Social Skills Intervention for Children with Autism *Emily A. Iobst, Laura A. Nabors, and Meghan E. McGrady*	71
Chapter 6	Effective School-Based Mental Health Interventions for Urban Youth *Dana Rofey, Laura Nabors and Irina Sumajin Parkins*	83
Chapter 7	Men's Ways of Mourning and their Implications for Psychological Counseling *Nehami Baum*	95
Index		111

PREFACE

Counseling psychology as a psychological specialty facilitates personal and interpersonal functioning across the life span with a focus on emotional, social, vocational, educational, health-related, developmental, and organizational concerns. Through the integration of theory, research, and practice, and with a sensitivity to multicultural issues, this specialty encompasses a broad range of practices that help people improve their well-being, alleviate distress and maladjustment, resolve crises, and increase their ability to live more highly functioning lives.

Though closely related to clinical psychology, counseling psychology differs from that field in a several subtle ways. First, counseling psychologists typically focus on less severe psychopathology (e.g., depression and anxiety), while clinical psychologists deal with more seriously disturbed individuals (e.g., those with schizophrenia or personality disorders). Second, counseling psychologists are more likely than clinical psychologists to assume a client-centered or humanistic theoretical approach. Finally, counseling psychology is unique in its attention both to normal developmental issues as well as the problems associated with physical, emotional, and mental disorders. Despite these differences, counseling and clinical psychology are becoming increasingly indistinguishable, leading some to suggest that these fields be combined.

Populations served by counseling psychologists include persons of all ages and cultural backgrounds. Examples of those populations would include late adolescents or adults with career/educational concerns and children or adults facing severe personal difficulties. Counseling psychologists also consult with organizations seeking to enhance their effectiveness or the well-being of their members.

Chapter 1 - This chapter reviews relevant prevention programs for couple distress and relationship violence, explores characteristics that couples and individuals value in such programs, and addresses the challenge of recruitment for prevention programs. Historically, psychological treatment has focused on the provision of services once an individual has manifested psychological difficulties, consistent with a medical pathological model. While secondary and tertiary interventions have met with some success in treating relationship distress and interpersonal violence, treatment outcome research indicates that these types of interventions are often less than adequate. Thus, increased attention has been given to the development of empirically validated prevention programs. For example, there is encouraging evidence that marital enhancement programs prevent relationship distress for up to 5 years following the intervention. Likewise, prevention programs for interpersonal violence have demonstrated positive changes in attitudes and behavioral intention to engage in aggressive behaviors immediately and over time.

The prevention approach, while promising, presents unique challenges to practitioners and interventionists, and psychological research in clinical psychology has begun to explore possible means to enhance the effectiveness of such programs. Research suggests that the individuals at highest risk of relationship distress and violence are often the least likely to seek out prevention programs. In response to such problems, researchers have examined those characteristics that couples and individuals value in such programs. Related research has examined variables that predict intention and participation in prevention programs for relationship distress and violence using a theoretical model of health-related behaviors, the Health Belief Model (HBM). This chapter will review research on characteristics that individuals state they value in prevention programs for relationships, and describe research predicting engaged couples' intentions and actual participation in premarital counseling programs and research predicting the behavioral intention to participate in prevention programming for interpersonal violence. Given the focus of clinical psychology on prevention, this chapter discusses an important line of research designed to ensure that prevention efforts for couples reach those who are most likely to benefit. Practical implications of this research are also discussed.

Chapter 2 - Objective: To assess the outcomes of a psycho-educational group intervention on the physical, mental, and social well-being of young women treated for breast cancer.

Background: Psycho-educational group interventions are evidence-based and focus on providing skills in coping, problem solving, and communication as well as information regarding cancer and its treatment. The authors approach was refined from information derived through focus groups and interviews with a similar group of 336 women.

Method: Young women (age 50 or less) were identified through the Rapid Case Ascertainment of the SEER Cancer Registry of the Greater San Francisco Bay Area (n=363). An experimental design with random assignment was used. The experimental condition was composed of 25 multi-ethnic groups, average size of 7.4 women that met for 10 weekly two-hour sessions. Analysis used a "Difference of a Difference model." Using an "intent to treat" approach, change was assessed between pre-post test and pre-6 months. Outcome measures were psychological and physical well-being. In addition to main effects, interactions with race/ethnicity, time since diagnosis, emotional support and previous counseling were included in the models.

Results: No main effects on psychological or physical measures of well-being were found for pre to post-test, albeit 88% of the experimental group found the intervention to be helpful. Interactions were found for positive effects of the intervention for women, who reported poorer emotional support, were a longer time since diagnosis (adjuvant therapy completed, except for tamoxifen), and who had previous counseling.

Discussion: Initially, women agreed to be randomized prior to knowing the day and location of the group's meetings. This resulted in a large number of women who never attended a group (n=60). One reason, the group intervention may not have been effective was that invidious comparisons between women in the group were made based on stage of disease and "downward comparisons" were not helpful. Alternatively, the support provided by "similar others" may have been less helpful. There is some evidence that intervention may have been too short to develop skills to resolve problems (those with prior counseling did better). Higher levels of mood dysphoria may have been due to the difficulties with maintaining denial. Findings from this study are consistent with those of Helgeson, 1999 and Antoni et al. 2001 whose populations and psychological intervention differed. The authors findings from subgroup analyses suggest that women who were emotionally needy benefited more from groups' psychological support.

Implications: Screen women for low social support and previous counseling and refer to group interventions. Hold groups at the end of treatment when they may be better prepared to take advantage of the skills training. Finally, a longer series or a second series of sessions may be needed.

Chapter 3 - The role of emergency departments (EDs) in providing patients with preventive services remains controversial; however, it is clear that vulnerable communities including minority, elderly and low income patients, seek out the ED for their primary medical care. For these vulnerable patient populations, the emergency department serves as a "safety net", providing essential health care needs to those most at risk patients, who may have limited or no access to regular medical services. For these at risk patients the emergency department can provide essential education on preventive health measures. Studies have demonstrated that, as part of their emergency care, patients both need and desire information on preventive health issues. While the arguments to provide health information and preventive services are persuasive there are legitimate barriers to providing these services in the emergency department such as time, responsibility and resources. The use of video as a tool for health education may help to diminish the barriers to effective health education for emergency department patients. Video offers several benefits over oral conveyance of information including: the consistency of information delivery, the ability to provide the tool in different languages, and the ability to utilize this method while the patient waits in the emergency department. Video effectiveness can also be enhanced as an educational tool by developing video interventions using a theoretical framework and a multidisciplinary approach. This approach can be used for any preventive care service that an emergency department patient population would need. This chapter will demonstrate how theory based educational videos can, and have been used successfully to educate emergency department patients, especially those with limited literacy or limited proficiency with the English language.

Chapter 4 - Ensuring that counselors-in-training learn the clinical skills necessary to be effective counselors prior to field placements is a major concern for faculty. This paper highlights how undergraduate volunteer clients can be utilized in the training of graduate students enrolled in an advanced counseling skills course. Results of this study demonstrate how effective this training modality was, with clients reporting a positive experience with the counseling sessions. Additionally, the counselors-in-training described the experience as realistic and more beneficial than role playing with a classmate. This data also demonstrates that clients can be helped with their difficulties in a rather short period of time by counselors-in-training. Recommendations for using this method, as well as limitations, are addressed.

Chapter 5 - This chapter outlines the theoretical background behind the social deficits evidenced in individuals with autism. Typical social interventions directed at improving social interaction for individuals with autism are discussed, and a newer intervention, the social story intervention, is discussed in detail. Research has shown that individuals with autism have an impaired or absent theory of mind – that is, they are typically unable to infer other people's thoughts and intentions from the social environment. The social story intervention intends to supply this information to the individual with autism in an individualized format in order to reduce targeted problem behavior or encourage appropriate behavior. Research, relying predominantly on case studies, has demonstrated that the social story intervention is, for the most part, moderately to highly effective in promoting appropriate social behavior. However, the research studies investigating this intervention have methodological weaknesses that must be remedied in future research, in order to make conclusive decisions regarding the effectiveness of the social story as an intervention.

Chapter 6 - Effective treatments are needed to improve mental health services for low-income, minority families. Transporting effective interventions to school-based mental health (SBMH) clinics may improve outcomes for children receiving services; however, implementation studies may be needed to measure the effectiveness of these interventions. Several programs are discussed that are empirically validated and successful in the community or in SBMH clinics. This chapter emphasizes important key components such as parental involvement, case management, children's empowerment, and mentoring to improve students' adjustment and achievement at school. Translating benefits of mental health services into gains valued by school administrators and teachers may improve acceptance of mental health services within schools. It is concluded that transporting and implementing interventions in SBMH clinics may improve children's academic, emotional and behavioral functioning and may provide valuable data for funding to ensure the growth of SBMH programs.

Chapter 7 - Based on the literature on loss and bereavement, this chapter will explore men's ways of mourning. Covering a range of losses through death (of a child, parent, spouse) and other events (divorce, immigration, wife's miscarriage), the chapter will discuss when, how, and what men mourn, in distinction from women. The chapter will argue that full recognition of men's losses in these instances, especially losses through non-death events, which tend to be disenfranchised in men, is an essential pre-requisite to offering men the emotional help they may need. It will also argue that since men mourn the losses differently from women, counselors must take their unique ways of mourning into consideration in their treatment of men. Finally, the chapter will offer practical suggestions on when and how to reach out with offers of help to men, on ways of facilitating the mourning process of men in therapy, and on issues to consider in the treatment termination with men.

Chapter 1

PREVENTION PROGRAMS FOR RELATIONSHIP DISTRESS AND VIOLENCE: IMPORTANCE, EXEMPLARS, AND STRATEGIES FOR RECRUITMENT

Tara L. Cornelius[1], Kieran T. Sullivan[2] and Ryan C. Shorey[1]
[1]Grand Valley State University, MI, USA
[2]Santa Clara University, CA, USA

ABSTRACT

This chapter reviews relevant prevention programs for couple distress and relationship violence, explores characteristics that couples and individuals value in such programs, and addresses the challenge of recruitment for prevention programs. Historically, psychological treatment has focused on the provision of services once an individual has manifested psychological difficulties, consistent with a medical pathological model. While secondary and tertiary interventions have met with some success in treating relationship distress and interpersonal violence, treatment outcome research indicates that these types of interventions are often less than adequate. Thus, increased attention has been given to the development of empirically validated prevention programs. For example, there is encouraging evidence that marital enhancement programs prevent relationship distress for up to 5 years following the intervention (Markman et al., 2006). Likewise, prevention programs for interpersonal violence have demonstrated positive changes in attitudes and behavioral intention to engage in aggressive behaviors immediately and over time (Avery-Leaf et al., 1997; Foshee et al., 2000, 2005).

The prevention approach, while promising, presents unique challenges to practitioners and interventionists, and psychological research in clinical psychology has begun to explore possible means to enhance the effectiveness of such programs. Research suggests that the individuals at highest risk of relationship distress and violence are often the least likely to seek out prevention programs (Sullivan and Bradbury, 1997). In response to such problems, researchers have examined those characteristics that couples and individuals value in such programs. Related research has examined variables that predict intention and participation in prevention programs for relationship distress and violence using a theoretical model of health-related behaviors, the Health Belief Model

(HBM). This chapter will review research on characteristics that individuals state they value in prevention programs for relationships, and describe research predicting engaged couples' intentions and actual participation in premarital counseling programs and research predicting the behavioral intention to participate in prevention programming for interpersonal violence. Given the focus of clinical psychology on prevention, this chapter discusses an important line of research designed to ensure that prevention efforts for couples reach those who are most likely to benefit. Practical implications of this research are also discussed.

INTRODUCTION

The need for interventions designed to prevent couple distress and violence has been made clear by the mixed findings in the couple treatment literature. We now know that the majority of distressed couples do not seek treatment and as many as half of treated couples remain unchanged or distressed at the end of therapy (Shadish and Baldwin, 2005). Long-term follow-up data indicate that about one-third of successfully treated couples relapse after 2 years (Christensen and Heavey, 1999). Further, research has suggested that even the most effective therapeutic approaches for treating marital distress have limited success and are very expensive (Albee, 1990; Van Widenfelt et al., 1997). In addition to the limited success of these programs, the experience of couple distress and marital dissolution is often associated with several serious physical and psychological consequences for both partners, including increased risk of psychopathology, increased incidence of physical illness, decreased longevity, and increased likelihood of suicidal ideation (Bloom, Asher, and White, 1978; Burman and Margolin, 1992; Schmoldt, Pope, and Hibbard, 1989). Marital distress is also associated with suppressed immune functioning, cardiovascular arousal, and increases in stress-related hormones (Gottman and Notarius, 2000).

Similarly, treatments for interpersonal violence after the individual is experiencing aggression in their relationship reveal that the majority relapse into the same problems at a later date (Griffing et al., 2002; Shurman and Rodriguez, 2006; Strube, 1988), many individuals fail to terminate violent relationships (Shurman and Rodriguez, 2006), and few individuals evidencing violence seek voluntary treatment, especially amongst certain ethnic groups (Ingram, 2007). Additionally, the presence of interpersonal violence is associated with a variety of negative psychological consequences, including lower self-esteem, reduced self-worth, increased self-blame, anger, hurt and anxiety (Jackson, Cram, and Seymour, 2000; Jezl, Molidor, and Wright, 1996; Nightingale and Morrissette, 1993; Smith and Donnelly, 2001; Truman-Schram, Cann, Calhoun, and Vanwallendael, 2000). Some researchers have also suggested that these early patterns may provide a potential trajectory toward more violence (Frieze, 2000; O'Leary et al., 1989; Prospero, 2006; Smith and Donnelly, 2001).

REVIEW OF PREVENTION PROGRAMS

On the basis of the limitations with secondary and tertiary interventions, increasingly clinicians and researchers are focusing less on intervention after couples are experiencing distress and more on *prevention* of distress prior to its development. The prevention approach may be advantageous in that it may be more successful than treatment regimes and the individual does not need to experience the problem behavior and the resulting negative correlates (Albee, 1990). In the area of relationship distress and interpersonal violence, several prevention programs have been empirically supported.

The Prevention and Relationship Enhancement Program (PREP) is arguably the most extensively researched premarital program designed to prevent distress and marital dissolution prior to its development (Markman, Stanley, and Blumberg, 1994). The underlying assumption of this approach is that if you teach happily engaged or married couples skills and problem-solving techniques their immediate satisfaction will increase, and they will be able to confront future marital crises appropriately, without resorting to divorce or experiencing significant relationship distress (Guerney, 1977; Powell and Wampler, 1982). The PREP program seeks to help the couple develop, refine, and integrate appropriate speaker and listener skills into their marital relationship in order to enhance and improve relationship satisfaction, both in the present and the future (Jacobson and Gurman, 1995; Markman, et al., 1994). This program has been extensively evaluated, and four- and five-year follow-up data suggest that couples who volunteered to participate in the program showed more positive affect, increased communication and problem solving behavior, and more support and validation than did control group couples. Additionally, the intervention couples were less likely to dissolve their relationships than the control couples or those couples who declined to participate in PREP (Markman, Renick, Floyd, Stanley, and Clements, 1993).

While these data strongly support the PREP program as leading to several positive marital outcomes, a criticism of these studies is their reliance on a homogenous group of individuals. To combat the limitation of these data, Stanley, Amato, Johnson and Markman (2006) examined the effect of premarital education programs on marital quality and stability within the general population, yielding more ethnically and economically diverse samples. Specifically, approximately 2000 married individuals across four U.S. states were included in this study, and participants were surveyed regarding their participation in premarital counseling, marital quality and stability, marital conflict, relationship commitment, history of divorce, and various demographic variables that are related to participation in premarital prevention programs and likelihood of divorce. The results of this study suggested that participation in premarital programming was significantly and positively associated with marital quality and relationship commitment, and significantly and negatively associated with marital conflict and divorce. In general, this study found few moderating effects of demographic or personal variables on the benefits of premarital programs, suggesting that the beneficial effects of these programs are relatively consistent across most married individuals. This study provides further evidence that premarital prevention programs are associated with positive marital outcomes and lower divorce rates, and encouraging couples in the general population to participate in such programs is a worthwhile endeavor for clinicians and researchers alike (Stanley, et al., 2006).

Several programs have also been implemented to prevent interpersonal violence in relationships. Although techniques and theoretical underpinnings vary, prevention can be broadly divided into two subtypes: primary and secondary prevention. Primary prevention programs aim to circumvent violence in dating relationship before it occurs, often through either targeting the entire population within a school, or utilizing data with regard to risk markers to present prevention programs to those individuals most likely to later become involved in violent intimate relationships. Primary prevention is achieved when the first instance of violence in dating relationships is precluded (Foshee, et al., 1996). In contrast, secondary prevention programs are designed to address violence that is already occurring in a relationship, and are successful when either the victims leave violent dating relationships or the perpetrator(s) cease initiating violence (Foshee, et al., 1996).

The Safe Dates Project, developed by Foshee et al. (1996, 1998, 2000, 2004), was designed to provide primary and secondary prevention of perpetration and victimization of dating violence in 8th and 9th grade adolescents. The theoretical framework for this program focused on changing dating violence norms, gender stereotyping, conflict-management skills, and particularly for those already involved in a violent relationship, altering the cognitive factors associated with help-seeking behavior. The initial wave of outcome data, collected one month after program activities, revealed 25% less psychological abuse perpetration, 60% less sexual perpetration, and 60% less physical violence perpetrated in the treatment schools than in the control schools. Additionally, treatment schools evidenced differences in the desired direction with regard to dating violence norms, gender stereotyping, and awareness of services available. In the primary prevention subsample, there was 28% less psychological abuse initiated in the treatment condition, and 27% less psychological abuse perpetration and 61% less sexual perpetration in the secondary prevention subsample of the treatment group, as compared to the control group. In order to examine the durability of the effects of the Safe Dates program, Foshee et al. (2000) presented additional follow-up data on 85% of the original sample, collected one year following the prevention project. The results of this follow-up study suggested that adolescents in the treatment group were less accepting of dating violence, perceived more negative consequences from engaging in dating violence, and were more aware of victim and perpetrator services. However, no significant differences were found at 1-year follow-up between the treatment and control groups on any of the behavioral outcomes. Additional follow-up was conducted at 4-years post-treatment on approximately 48% of the original sample (Foshee, et al., 2004), and revealed that adolescents in the treatment condition reported significantly less physical, serious physical, and sexual perpetration and victimization, suggesting the long-term durability of self-reported reductions in perpetration and victimization associated with the Safe Dates Project.

Avery-Leaf and colleagues (1997) implemented a five-session prevention curriculum intended to change attitudinal correlates of dating violence. The specific goals of the program included promoting equity in dating relationships by highlighting the deleterious effects of inequality, challenging the conceptualization of violence as an acceptable conflict resolution tactic, encouraging constructive communication, and increasing knowledge of resources available for victims of dating violence. The results from this study demonstrated that both males and females in the treatment group were significantly less accepting of aggression in the context of a dating relationship compared to pre-treatment levels, and that this effect was not evident for the control group. These data suggest that participation in prevention programming resulted in changes in the attitudinal correlates of dating aggression.

SPECIAL ISSUES FOR PREVENTION

From the above discussion, it should be evident that prevention programming for relationship distress and violence has shown promise in altering current and future negative interpersonal behaviors and preventing the development of distress and abuse.

Although progress in the development and evaluation of prevention programs is indeed encouraging, the effective use of these programs is limited, in part, by a lack of effective recruitment strategies. How do we target individuals who are likely to benefit, and how do we encourage them to seek out such programming? Participation in voluntary prevention programs in community samples is relatively low (Sullivan and Bradbury, 1997). In addition, prevention programs are often initiated without regard to the particular population to be targeted. Even the most efficacious programs are unlikely to be successful if they are not attended by those who are likely to benefit. Several researchers have noted that programs designed to prevent marital distress are not likely to be attended by those most in need. Silliman and Schumm (1995) surveyed never married college students about their beliefs related to premarital counseling, and found that those who were most likely to experience later problems tended to be reticent to attend, despite being a group that would receive the most benefit from such prevention. Similarly, Sullivan and Bradbury (1997) retrospectively asked newlywed couples if they had participated in premarital counseling. Couples who had participated were compared to those who did not on a variety of known risk factors for marital distress. The results of this research suggested that there was no evidence that couples who participated in premarital prevention programs were at higher risk for marital distress. Rather, most often, couples who received the prevention program tended to be at relatively low risk for marital discord (Sullivan and Bradbury). Halford et al. (2006) confirmed these findings with a sample of 374 newlywed couples, and found that couples who were at relatively high risk for marital problems were underrepresented in premarital programs. Additionally, ineffective recruitment may result in biased sampling in efficacy studies, thus leading to inaccurate data on the clinical significance of these programs.

Therefore, empirically examining factors related to recruitment for prevention programs is a fruitful and useful direction for researchers in clinical psychology. The remainder of this chapter is devoted to discussing recent research on valued characteristics and directions for recruitment for prevention programs within the field of interpersonal relationships, specifically preventing marital distress and interpersonal violence.

PROGRAM CHARACTERISTICS

Two studies were designed to examine those factors of premarital prevention programs that are attractive to potential participants (see Sullivan and Anderson, 2002 and Duncan and Wood, 2003). Most premarital prevention programs are developed rationally, based on what the clinician or researcher believes is most important in terms of preventing relationship distress and dissolution. However, these factors may or may not be the characteristics that potential participants find appealing. Therefore, these studies were designed to determine characteristics of premarital prevention programs that are perceived as most important to young adults and newlywed couples. Additionally, these studies allowed some examination of how those factors that attract individuals to premarital programs may differ for high risk versus lower risk couples.

Study 1

Sullivan and Anderson (2002) used two samples to help identify the program characteristics that are attractive to potential participants. This study was designed to collect preliminary data on those facets of premarital prevention programs that were important to newlyweds who may or may not have participated in premarital counseling, with the goal of creating a measure for use with engaged couples. Since few studies have systematically examined factors that make premarital programs attractive to potential participants, phase one of this study involved conducting focus groups with newlywed couples. Thirty two newlyweds (16 couples), some of whom had participated in premarital counseling and others who did not, met in focus groups to discuss factors that attracted them (or would have attracted them) to premarital counseling programs and those factors that discouraged them (or would have discouraged them). The couples were recruited through newspaper advertisements and flyers, and ranged in age from 20 to 54. Participants qualified for the focus groups if they were married less than 1 year and spoke English. Four focus groups were conducted and were designed to bring together individuals into relatively homogeneous groups, a traditional strategy in focus group research (Morgan and Scannell, 1998). During the focus groups, couples were asked to discuss a series of questions about premarital counseling and were paid for their participation. The focus group data was then transcribed and coded by undergraduate research assistants. These data suggested four broad categories of important characteristics identified by the focus groups: leader characteristics, setting, content, and evidence of positive outcomes. Based on these data, individual items related to each of these domains were created for a questionnaire designed to assess how important each of the specific characteristics of premarital counseling would be in helping individuals decide on attending premarital prevention programs. The reliability of this measure was adequate (Cronbach's alpha = .70 for men and .68 for women).

Phase two of this study involved evaluating this questionnaire with engaged couples in combination with other measures designed to assess the individual's risk for later marital distress. Engaged couples were recruited through flyers at bridal stores, newspaper advertisements, and in person at bridal shows. Couples were eligible for the study if they were engaged, their wedding date was at least 6 months away, and they had not yet participated in premarital counseling. Eighty-six engaged couples (age range from 19 to 60) were surveyed via mail with the constructed measure assessing the four general domains identified by the focus groups. Participants were also encouraged to identify additional topics that they thought would be beneficial in premarital prevention programs. In addition, couples completed a series of questions designed to assess their level of risk for later distress and marital dissolution, which were based on research suggesting that younger couples with lower income and educational levels, who are more neurotic, and have cohabitated before marriage are at higher risk of future marital problems (Karney and Bradbury, 1995; Larson and Holman, 1994; Kelly and Conley, 1987). Engaged partners completed and mailed the measures independently, and when both partners' packets were received, they were paid for their participation.

The results of this study revealed that some aspects of premarital prevention programs were perceived as very important. Consistent with other research (Silliman, Schumm, and Jurich, 1992), couples valued working with a trustworthy, experienced, and professional leader and content that was insight-oriented and educational in nature. To a lesser degree, the perceived usefulness of the program by past participants, the convenience of the program such as location, and the amount of time investment were also considered important. Men and women's perceptions of the important characteristics were highly similar, with the exception of the characteristic of insight-oriented counseling. This feature was significantly more important to women than to men. Interestingly, several factors were not important to the majority of couples. Specifically, couples did not rate practicing skills, role play, or group discussions, nor characteristics of the leader(s) (i.e., gender and individual vs. couple), as important.

Differences of perceived importance of the characteristics between high risk and low risk couples were found based on gender and risk level for future marital problems. For men, those with lower education (presumed to be at higher risk) tended to rate the inclusion of practice and role-playing as more important. Higher risk women tended to be less likely to rate having a professional, trustworthy leader and an educational content as important, and were more likely to rate having a group format and discussing issues with other couples as important.

Study 2

Duncan and Wood (2003) conducted a similar study with undergraduates who had never been married. This study was also designed to examine factors that were important in motivating individuals to participate in premarital prevention programming, and how these factors may vary depending on the individual's family-related risk for divorce and distress. In order to guide the research, the *4 P's* of marketing (Katz, 1988) were used as a conceptual framework, which contends that product, price, place and promotion are important in marketing a professional service. The product component includes all aspects related to the service being provided, and that the individuals perceive themselves vulnerable to the problem, and that the product is a reasonable solution to that problem. Price involves both the monetary and intangible aspects of the cost of the product, including time, effort, self-disclosure, etc. The place component is the physical (or cyber) location of the service, and it is probable that convenience of the place is particularly important for individuals in predicting their participation. Finally, promotion involves the means of marketing or bringing awareness of the service to the potential participant, which could include advertising, promotions, public relations, recommendations, or word of mouth.

Based on these four aspects, a questionnaire was designed to assess factors likely to affect the decision to participate in marriage preparation within this conceptual framework. The product area assessed various elements of the premarital prevention program itself, such as format, leaders, and instructional methods. With regard to the price aspect, both monetary and time cost was assessed. The place component was assessed through questions regarding distance and possible physical locations. Promotion was assessed through asking several questions about possible sources for learning about the program, such as a friend, church/temple, recently married couple, etc. Cronbach's alpha for each of these subscales were adequate. Motivation to participate was assessed through a four-item scale.

Nine-hundred sixty four never married undergraduates completed this measure in addition to answering questions about family risk factors for marital distress and divorce. Specifically, participants were asked about their parental marital relationship, parental divorce, and about their familial harmony. The results of this study suggested that individuals were equally likely to attend regardless of parental divorce, marital unhappiness, or disharmonious family environment. However, this effect appears to be moderated by gender and optimism about marriage. Specifically, females were more motivated to participate than males, and males with parental divorce evidenced higher motivation to participate. Also, individuals experiencing parental divorce and unhappiness and females reporting unhappy family environment reported less optimism about marriage, and thus, lower motivation to attend premarital counseling. This suggests that those that are at higher risk due to their familial history are less likely to engage in marital-maintaining behaviors even at the premarital level.

With regard to the *4 P's*, both higher risk and lower risk groups reported a preference for well-trained and respectful leaders, although those with higher risk reported less interest in group formats and those led by clergy. Additionally, those with greater risk were less likely to report being motivated to participate in programs recommended by their parents or clergy. Related to the price component, males with lower family climate reported higher willingness to invest more time and money into premarital prevention programming. In terms of the place component, there was a small preference for prevention programming in churches or temples, although among those reporting parental divorce or unhappiness there was lower preference for this setting. With regard to promotion, there was little difference between the two risk groups (Duncan and Wood, 2003).

Implications of these Data

There are several practical implications of these data for prevention programming and participant recruitment. One of the most robust findings from Study 1 is that characteristics of the leader are particularly important in the couples' perception of the features of the prevention programs that are most important. In terms of recruitment, these data suggest that emphasizing the leader's credentials, experience, expertise, and ethical principles may be useful in recruiting couples to participate. Additionally, educational content of the program was perceived as important to most couples in this study. This suggests that recruitment efforts should emphasize the educational facets of the program at least in the initial stages of recruitment. Practically, this may involve actually marketing programs as "education" rather than "counseling", since this may be more consistent with the important characteristics of engaged couples. However, given the gender difference in the relative importance of insight-oriented prevention programs, and also recognizing that women are often the ones to initiate couples interventions (Doss, Atkins, and Christensen, 2003), it may make sense to at least acknowledge insight-oriented strategies included in the program minimally in initial recruitment of couples.

Additionally, several engaged couples identified effectiveness as an important feature of prevention programs. Therefore, it may be useful to provide some data regarding the effectiveness of the program, including outcome data conducted in the community setting. Unfortunately, the data from Study 1 did not provide clear data regarding differences in characteristics deemed important for high risk and lower risk couples. This is due in part to the variability in responses for these groups between men and women, with women showing more variability in responses based on their higher risk status. Therefore, from these data, we are not able to identify specific recruitment strategies that are effective *only* for higher risk couples, but this study does give us some indication as to factors important generally for couples of varying risk levels, as noted above (Sullivan and Anderson, 2002).

Study 2 provides interesting information regarding how familial risk factors may impact motivation to participate in premarital counseling programs. Amongst those evidencing greater familial risk, there is less optimism about their future marital relationship, and it appears, in turn, less motivation to participate in premarital prevention. This suggests that perhaps one way to intervene for young adults is to alter one's optimism about their marital relationship, which may then, presumably, increase one's willingness to seek out marital preparation programs. It may be possible to enhance optimism about marriage for young adults through exposure to marital successes and through cognitive restructuring about possible deterministic misconceptions individuals harbor related to their familial history and their marital relationship (Duncan and Wood, 2003). An interesting finding from this study show that despite this reduced optimism and particularly amongst males, individuals reporting higher risk are willing to spend more time and money on premarital prevention and are more tolerant of possible negative characteristics of the leader. Therefore, it seems that individuals with familial risk recognize their personal vulnerability, but it may be that this is insufficient to alter behavior in the context of the reduced optimism about their future marital relationships.

Additionally, individuals with familial risk are less likely to be motivated to attend programs conducted by or recommended by parents or clergy, or to attend those in church settings. Given their parental and family interactions, it would make sense that these individuals would be reticent to rely on recommendations from their parents, and may desire feedback and counseling independently and from other sources. With regard to the reduced preference for religiously-affiliated leaders and locations, it is possible that individuals with higher risk may be alienated from their religious community, or may be reticent to participate in such affiliated programs if such programs strongly discourage divorce. This suggests that for those with higher risk, it may be more useful to conduct premarital prevention programs in religiously neutral locations to encourage those individuals to attend and fully participate (Duncan and Wood, 2003).

PREDICTING INTENTION AND PARTICIPATION IN PREVENTION PROGRAMS

While the above studies provide some useful information as to the factors related to prevention programs that were valued in couples and individuals, it is not necessarily clear how well those actually predict intention and participation in such programming. Therefore, additional research has sought to clarify how different beliefs and attitudes about prevention programs relate to participation. In order to provide a unifying framework for examination of factors likely to influence one's decision to participate, a theoretical model of preventative behaviors was used in much of this research to guide the development of the measures and frame analyses.

The Health Belief Model

A theoretical model of health-related behaviors, the Health Belief Model (HBM), is a value-expectancy theory that provides a useful framework for examining factors relating to participation in preventative behaviors (Rosenstock, 1966). The HBM posits that a variety of factors in combination affect a person's self-reported likelihood to participate in prevention efforts. The HBM model includes four factors: perceived susceptibility, perceived severity, perceived barriers, and perceived benefits. Specifically, individuals are more likely to engage in preventive behaviors if they perceive that they are susceptible to the potential problem, they believe the problem to have severe consequences, they perceive few barriers to participating, and they perceive the program to be beneficial. The factor structure of the HBM has been examined and suggests that the dimensions are discrete enough to be considered different beliefs (Jette, Cummings, Brock, Phelps, and Naessens, 1981), and have been found to predict preventative behavior in a variety of domains, including contraceptive use, mammograms, medication compliance, and breast self-examination, to name a few (Eisen and Zellman, 1986; Hyman and Baker, 1992; Ronis and Harel, 1989; Strecher, Champion, and Rosenstock, 1997). Therefore, this theoretical model may provide a useful framework for understanding individuals' willingness to participate in prevention programming for relationship distress and interpersonal violence.

Study 1

Sullivan, Pasch, Cornelius and Cirigliano (2004) conducted a study examining couples' intention and actual participation in prevention programs for relationship distress using the four HBM factors: perceived susceptibility, perceived severity, perceived barriers, and perceived benefits. In addition to these four facets, this study also examined how participants' intention and participation was influenced by important others in their lives, as well as knowledge factors related to the problem, since these have been shown in other literatures to predict health behaviors (Morrison, Baker, and Gillmore, 2000; Strecher et al., 1997).

Based on the content of the focus groups conducted in a previous study (Sullivan and Anderson, 2002, described above), a 36-item questionnaire assessing knowledge, the influence of significant others, and the four aspects of the HBM model was designed, which was modeled after a questionnaire designed to assess the HBM factors predicting mammography use in women (Aiken et al., 1994). Knowledge items assessed awareness of current divorce rates in the U. S., the stages of marriage when divorce is most likely, and the percent of couples who consider divorce (4 items). A social norms scale was designed to assess the influence of significant individuals on attending premarital prevention programming, and asked if the participants knew of people who had attended or recommended counseling, and whether they found it helpful (4 items). The four HBM scales were rationally developed based on the content of the focus groups and examined with a confirmatory factor analysis, and resulted in a final questionnaire of 6 items assessing perceived susceptibility of divorce and marital problems, 4 items assessing perceived severity of marital problems, 5 items measuring perceived barriers, and 4 items measuring perceived benefits. All items were scaled on a 5-point Likert scale and verbally anchored at each end. Scale scores were calculated by summing the scores for each of the individual items making up the scale. Cronbach's alpha for each of the HBM was adequate for men and women. Behavioral intention to participate was assessed through a rating as to the percentage chance that they would choose to participate in premarital prevention programming.

Within the context of the HBM model, this study examined couples intention (Time 1) and then subsequent behavior of engaging in premarital counseling (Time 2), while controlling for relevant demographic variables and if counseling was required or recommended at Time 2. The recruitment strategies and the inclusionary criteria were the same as in Study 1 described above. At Time 1, the sample of 86 couples were sent the HBM questionnaire including the knowledge and the social norms subscales, and instructed to complete the measure and send it back independent of their partner. When both partners returned their questionnaire, they were paid for their participation. At Time 2, each participant was contacted by phone approximately one month after their wedding. Approximately 88% of the original sample participated in the Time 2 data. Spouses completed the interviews separately, and were asked whether they had participated in premarital counseling and if such participation was required. The majority of couples indicated that participation at Time 1 did not influence their behavior at Time 2, and in the minority of cases in which participants said that Time 1 influenced Time 2, they also indicated that counseling was required by the church that performed their wedding.

The results of this study suggested that at Time 1, the HBM factors significantly predicted intention after controlling for demographic variables, accounting for an additional 23% of variance for women and 19% for men. For women, susceptibility to marital problems and divorce and perceived barriers were significant predictors. For men, only barriers (specifically the barrier related to expense) emerged as a significant predictor after controlling for other variables. Social norms also emerged as a significant predictor of intention after controlling for significant demographic variables, accounting for an additional 3% and 7% of variance for women and men, respectively. For both women and men, having respected people recommend counseling was a significant predictor, although peer benefits were not.

At Time 2, examining the actual behavior of individuals, approximately 60% of couples reported received premarital prevention programming. The majority of couples reported that the counseling they received was related to a church organization and that it was required. Therefore, the data analytic strategy was designed to control for whether counseling was required or recommended and to determine what predicted behavior after taking these factors into account. The same individual predictors that were correlated with intention were also correlated with actual participation (i.e., age for men, income for women, and barriers, benefits, and recommendations for men and women). Men and women's earlier intention to participate was significantly correlated to their actual participation in premarital counseling. Logistic regression equations suggested that intention to participate significantly predicted participation after controlling for whether counseling was required or recommended, as did perceived barriers for men. For women, required participation was a significant predictor as was perceived barriers, although barriers did not significantly predict after controlling for whether counseling was required. For men and women, recommendations by respected people significantly predicted participation after controlling for whether participation was required, and accounted for an additional 15% and 9% of variance, respectively.

Implications of these Data

Although given that the majority of couples were required to participate in premarital prevention programs, thus limiting the variability in other factors in predicting intention, several implications of these data can be identified. First, the data in this study suggest that the factors that predict variability in participation in premarital prevention programs are identifiable and can inform dissemination efforts. Although data from Time 1 suggested that women's intention to participate was influenced by perceived susceptibility and perceived severity, this was not the case for men, and neither of these HBM factors predicted actual participation. This suggests that commonly used "scare tactics" that are designed to emphasize one's individual susceptibility or the severity of the problem are not likely to work effectively to change the *behavior* of couples. One consistent finding in this study was the effect of perceived barriers in predicting intention and participation. This suggests that recruitment that focuses on reduction of perceived barriers may effectively increase couples motivation to participate in premarital counseling. Specifically, reducing the cost, making counseling convenient, and increasing couples' perception that the leader is trustworthy and competent may assist in recruitment efforts. The most robust finding from this study was the predictive utility of counseling being recommended by someone respected by the couple. Therefore, ensuring that respected professionals are recommending premarital counseling may be a very effective strategy to ensure that couples are seeking out such preventative programs. Particularly for couples without a strong connection to a religious organization for whom counseling may not be required, recommendations by respected individuals would be particularly important. In addition to clergy, who are often respected leaders and counselors for individuals involved in religious communities, mental health workers, doctors, politicians, and others who hold respected positions in the community may be able to assist in ensuring couples have access to important preventative programs to circumvent marital distress and divorce and avoid the negative psychological and physical consequences therein (Sullivan, Pasch, Cornelius and Cirigliano, 2004).

Study 2

Cornelius, Sullivan, Resseguie, and Milliken (in press) examined factors related to the behavioral intention to participate in prevention programs for dating violence. Given the recent interest in prevention programming for interpersonal violence occurring in dating relationships (Foshee et al., 2005; Whitaker et al., 2006), examining these factors is crucial in the development of programs that specifically target those variables most important to the individuals who are most likely to need such training, and improve our ability to recruit high risk individuals. To date, no other empirical research has examined factors related to participation in prevention programs for dating violence. Like the previous study, the HBM model was used in the construction of a measure to assess these factors and to frame analyses. Based on previous findings, this research hypothesized that the HBM factors would significantly predict intention to participate in prevention programs for dating violence over and above relevant demographic variables. It was further hypothesized that self-reported aggression would be related to the HBM factors and that the relationship between beliefs and intention may vary based on aggression. Specifically, it was hypothesized that physical and psychological aggression would be positively related to perceived susceptibility and perceived benefits, and negatively related to perceived barriers.

Participants were recruited through the introductory psychology research pool at a large, public, Midwestern university. Participants qualified for the study if they indicated a current or previous dating relationship, defined as planned, social, romantic, or intimate activity with another individual. One hundred eighty ($N = 180$) undergraduate psychology students qualified and participated in the study. Participants completed a brief demographic measure and the Conflict Tactics Scale-II (CTS-II; Straus, Hamby, Boney-McCoy, and Sugarman, 1996), which was used to assess rates of physical and psychological aggression that occurred in an intimate relationship, including both perpetration and victimization. Participants also completed the Relationship Beliefs and Attitudes Questionnaire (RBA), which was a 24-item self-report measure adapted from the measure used in Sullivan, Pasch, Cornelius and Cirigliano (2004), and was designed to assess beliefs about dating violence and programs designed to prevent dating violence. This measure conceptualized participation in prevention programs as a health related preventative behavior, using the HBM as a guide, and assessed perceived susceptibility ($n = 3$), perceived severity of dating violence ($n = 8$), perceived barriers to participation ($n = 6$), and perceived benefits ($n = 7$). Unlike the study conducted by Sullivan, Pasch, Cornelius, and Cirigliano (2004), knowledge and social norms were not included, since preliminary data with this sample suggested overall low knowledge of dating violence and virtually no respected or peer recommendations for prevention programming. Three items assessed the behavioral intention to participate in a prevention program for dating violence, which were summed to provide a score of behavioral intention.

A confirmatory factor analysis resulted in modifications of the RBA to include two severity scales (perceived severity of verbal aggression and perceived severity of physical aggression). The model was further modified by eliminating three items from the barriers scale and one item from the susceptibility scale which did not load significantly on their respective scales. The barrier items were retained for individual analysis as they appeared to be potentially important, albeit conceptually different, barriers to intention to participate. For the modified five-factor model, CFI = .94 and RMSEA = .075, indicating a good fit. Scale scores were calculated for each participant by summing the scores of the individual HBM items making up the scale for each factor. Cronbach's alpha for each of the four HBM models and the intention scale were acceptable.

The results from this study suggested that perceived susceptibility and perceived benefits significantly predicted intention after controlling for demographic variables in the expected direction; that is, participants who perceived themselves as more susceptible to future dating violence and participants who perceived greater benefits to participation were more likely to intend to participate in a program designed to prevent dating violence. Two of the barrier items that had not loaded on the barriers scale were significant predictors of intentions. The convenience of the program and concerns about learning something about the relationship that participants did not want to know accounted for an additional 14% and 6% of the variance, respectively, after controlling for income and gender. As would be expected, the more inconvenient a program is perceived, the lower the intention to participate. Curiously, the more the individual perceived that the program would reveal things about them that they did not want to know, the higher the intention to participate.

Because this sample included both those who reported no violence in their dating relationships (i.e., a primary prevention sample), and those who did report violence in their relationship (i.e., a secondary prevention sample), differences in beliefs and the relationship to intention were examined. Thirty-eight percent of the participants reported experiencing physical aggression in their relationships (N = 69) and 83% reported that they had experienced psychological aggression in their relationships (N = 149). Only two of the 69 participants who reported experiencing physical aggression reported experiencing no psychological aggression. Consistent with previous research, the rates of bidirectionality were very high for both types of violence. Among those reporting psychological aggression, 95% of participants reported both perpetration and victimization of psychological aggression. Among those reporting physical violence, 70% reported both perpetration and victimization of physical violence. Thus, perpetration and victimization were analyzed simultaneously for this sample.

In order to evaluate whether physical and psychological aggression were related to HBM factors, zero-order correlations were conducted. Perceived susceptibility was positively correlated with psychological and physical violence, such that the more psychological or physical violence, the more participants perceived themselves as susceptible to future dating violence. The perceived barriers scale was positively correlated with psychological aggression, such that the more psychological aggression experienced, the more participants perceived barriers to attending prevention programming. The perceived barriers scale was not significantly correlated with physical violence. The individual barrier item, inconvenience of the program, was negatively related to psychological and physical violence, suggesting that the more violence one experiences, the less inconvenient participation seems. Finally, concerns about learning something about your relationship that you do not want to know was positively correlated with psychological and physical violence. Thus, it appears that relationship violence is related to increased concerns about prevention programs revealing unwanted information about the relationship.

To determine whether intentions to participate in prevention programming varied based on the history of psychological or physical violence, two independent-samples t-tests were conducted. There were no significant differences in intention between participants who had experienced psychological aggression and participants who had not, nor between participants who had experience physical violence and participants who had not (Cornelius, Sullivan, Resseguie, and Milliken, in press).

Implications of these Data

Several important implications for recruitment for dating violence prevention programs emerge from these data. The individual HBM factors that predicted intention were perceived susceptibility and perceived benefits. Therefore, if we want to encourage individuals to participate in voluntary prevention programming for dating violence, we need to be emphasizing one's individual susceptibility and the benefits of the program. Specifically, it may be important to inform potential participants of the surprisingly high prevalence of dating violence and emphasize personal and relationship risk factors, in addition to explaining possible benefits, including encouraging non-violent communication, problem-solving skills for current or potential relationship problems, and improving current and future relationships. In addition, the individual barrier items suggest that minimizing perceived inconvenience of the program by making it accessible in time and place, reducing cost, and reducing effort necessary for participation will also increase participation. A significant correlation emerged between psychological aggression and the belief that participation in prevention programming would result in revealing something about one's relationship that the individual does not want to know and this item predicted intention, which is particularly interesting. This is an unexpected finding, since we had conceptualized this as a potential barrier to participation. In combination with the correlation data demonstrating that this item was also positively related to physical victimization and psychological victimization and perpetration, it may be that individuals engaging in violent behaviors recognize the problematic nature of their behavior and understand that prevention programs are likely to reveal these problems, but also recognize that participation in such programs is important and/or necessary for them. If we conceptualize those who report psychological violence as a group at risk for physical violence and thus a potentially fruitful target for primary prevention, these data suggest that focusing on these factors in recruitment may encourage those who may be at future risk for physical aggression to participate.

In terms of specifically targeting primary and secondary prevention samples for recruitment, several implications of these data emerge. Interestingly, no significant differences in intention were found between the violent and nonviolent groups. Participants were equally likely to intend to participate in prevention programming whether or not they had been experiencing psychological and/or physical violence in their relationships. This appears to contradict earlier findings in the marital literature that at risk individuals are less likely to participate in prevention programs than individuals who are not at risk (Halford et al. 2006; Sullivan & Bradbury, 1997). This apparent contradiction may be explained, however, by considering the relationships between violence and beliefs. Psychological aggression was significantly correlated with increased perceived susceptibility, perceived barriers, increased belief that prevention programs would reveal things about one's relationship that they did not want to know, and decreased perceived inconvenience of the program. Those who had experienced physical violence in their relationships also perceived themselves to be more susceptible to violence in their relationship. Physical violence was also related to higher individual perceived barriers items. Thus it appears that at-risk individuals hold various beliefs that may differentially affect intention. On one hand, they perceive higher susceptibility to violence and more benefits to participation which increases their intention to participate. On the other hand, they perceive more barriers to participation which decreases their intention to participate. Thus any between-group differences in intentions may be washed out by these various beliefs (Cornelius, Sullivan, Resseguie, and Milliken, in press).

GENERAL DISCUSSION

Taken together, what general themes can be identified from these four studies in terms of findings, implications, and future research directions? First, these studies represent initial steps in an important line of research, and the findings here are decidedly preliminary. Taken together, a picture is beginning to emerge of the factors that influence individuals and couples to participate in preventative programs for relationship distress and interpersonal violence. It is our hope that this chapter will inspire more researchers to begin investigating this important aspect of psychological prevention programming. Without effective recruitment strategies to target individuals who are likely to benefit and are in need of the prevention, it is of no matter if the treatment is efficacious. Even the most efficacious treatments are not useful in the absence of effective recruitment strategies to attract potential participants. Recognizing the preliminary and exploratory nature of the above studies, there are some general themes and findings worth noting.

First, both studies examining factors valued by potential participants suggested that respected, trustworthy leaders were important characteristics, and recommendations from a respected individual predicted both intention and behavior. In the study examining interpersonal violence, social norms and respected recommenders were assessed, and virtually no participants reported *any* recommendations for prevention programming. What this tells us is that for married and engaged couples, leaders and respected perceived authority figures are important sources of influence, and should be utilized in encouraging and recruiting participants. Therefore, enlisting these individuals in advocating and dissemination of the importance of prevention programming may be a useful strategy of recruitment for couples broadly. Interestingly, for engaged and married couples, peer recommendations and report of peer benefit did not predict intention or participation, suggesting that it is something about a trustworthy, respected leader in the community that is most influential in encouraging participation. For prevention programs for interpersonal violence, it is not clear if the role of authority and peer figures is the same, since there was a profound floor effect. From these data, it appears that no one is talking to adolescents and young adults about the possibility of attending prevention programs for dating violence. This is disconcerting, since a significant proportion of adolescents and young adults are reporting dating violence, and it is likely that prevention programming would reduce or prevent such outcomes. Assuming that the data regarding couples could apply to dating populations, it would perhaps be a useful strategy to at least increase the amount of peer and respected leader recommendations to determine if this is influential in encouraging participation in prevention programs and at the very minimum inform individuals that such programming may be available. This may also be appropriate for individuals with familial risk factors for distress and divorce, as suggested by the Duncan and Wood (2003) study. Given that the peer group is often a very important source of influence at the developmental period in which individuals may begin dating or first experience dating violence, it may be that this will be a powerful source of influence in recruiting participation. However, given the current data, it is not clear if such recommendations will increase participation, but giving adolescents and young adults such information about prevention is unlikely to do any harm.

With regard to the HBM factors, barriers as a group predicted intention and participation in premarital programs, and the individual barrier item of inconvenience predicted intention to participate in dating violence prevention. Taken together, designing programs to minimize perceived barriers such as inconvenience, cost, location, etc. may be a relatively straightforward way to improve participation. Perceived susceptibility predicted intention for the dating violence sample and for women's intention to participate in premarital counseling, although it did not emerge as a significant predictor of behavior for the engaged and married couples. Although value expectancy models of human behavior, including the HBM, posit that the best predictor of behavior is the individual's intention to perform the behavior (Morrison, Baker, Gillmore, 2000), it may be that perceived susceptibility increases perceived intention, but it does not subsequently affect actual behavior. It is also worth noting that the vast majority of individuals in our sample did not perceive themselves to be very susceptible to this problem. Overall, scores of susceptibility were low, but when an individual did perceive higher susceptibility, they rated their intention to participate in prevention programming as higher. It is also the case that the item, originally conceptualized as a barrier, of revealing things that you do not want to know, seemed to function like a susceptibility item, in that it increased intention to participate. It may be that individuals who perceived that prevention programming would reveal something that they did not want to know recognized their own susceptibility and need for prevention programming for dating violence. It is not clear whether perceived susceptibility or this item would have remained a significant predictor of actual behavior for those in the dating violence sample. It may be that perceived susceptibility increases one's belief that they *would* attend, as we saw with the women in the engaged couples, but that when it comes time to engage in the behavior, other factors, such as barriers, are stronger predictors.

Perceived benefits emerged as a significant predictor for the dating violence sample, but not for the engaged and married couples. However, in Sullivan and Anderson (2002), potential participants noted that data regarding the effectiveness of the program was important, which can be conceptualized as a benefit of the program. It may be that this failed to emerge as a significant factor for the HBM premarital study because the vast majority of participants were required to participate in premarital counseling, so the variance left to be explained by the other factors was limited. Therefore, it is difficult to discern if benefits is universally not an important factor in predicting intention and actual behavior with regard to premarital prevention programs, or if the nature of the sample prohibited examining such an effect. Regardless, the dating violence sample suggests that presenting data explaining possible benefits, including encouraging non-violent communication, solving current or potential relationship problems appropriately, and improving current and future relationships may assist in recruiting individuals and couples. Related, the dating violence study also provided some important information regarding the presence of the problem behavior and how this affects an individual's intention to participate. Perceived susceptibility was positively correlated with psychological and physical violence, such that the more psychological or physical violence, the more participants perceived themselves as susceptible to future dating violence. These data are important for recruitment in that it suggests that we should be cognizant of the individual's degree to which they are already experiencing the target behaviors of the prevention programming in recruitment, such that this may affect their willingness to engage in the prevention programming. Applying these data to prevention programs for relationship distress, it may be that for individuals who are already experiencing distress in their relationships, susceptibility of experiencing the problem may be an important consideration, although it may not be as important for those who are relatively satisfied at the time of the prevention program. In addition, concerns about learning something about your relationship that you do not want to know was positively correlated with psychological and physical violence. Thus, it appears that relationship violence is related to increased concerns about prevention programs revealing unwanted information about the relationship. It may be for individuals already engaging in the problem behavior, this concern may be present *and* there is a recognition of the necessity of the treatment. Exploring the nature of these beliefs may be a fruitful discussion within the context of the prevention program itself.

CONCLUSION

This research provides an important first step in examining factors related to recruitment for prevention programs for relationship distress and dating violence, an area that has been relatively neglected to date by both literatures. As practitioners and researchers move toward a prevention model of addressing psychological and psychosocial problems, empirically examining our methods for recruitment is increasingly important to ensure that those most likely to benefit are receiving the programming. It is our hope that this line of research will inspire further inquiries into aspects of individual's behavior that predict intention and participation in prevention programming. Clearly, further research is necessary to determine which of the HBM factors are predicting intention and behavior for what types of prevention programs, and perhaps more importantly, why these factors are important. Additionally, other theoretical models, such as the theory of reasoned action (Fishbein and Ajzen, 1975), may also provide useful additions to understanding the variability in intention and actual behavior, as well as idiosyncratic differences between individuals.

The dating violence study described in this chapter was a first step in examining differences between primary prevention, targeted prevention for those at higher risk, and secondary prevention. Further research is necessary to understand those factors that predict intention and behavior in light of the individual's risk for certain behaviors that are the target of the prevention program. For example, further research is necessary examining factors that uniquely predict intention to participate for victims and perpetrators individually, in addition to those engaging in mutual violence. Given that research suggests that a significant proportion of individuals in relationships are both recipients and perpetrators of aggressive behavior (Gray and Foshee, 1997; Bookwala, Frieze, Smith, and Ryan, 1992; Cate, Henton, Koval, Christopher, and Lloyd, 1982), it may be that cases of mutual violence necessitate specialized recruitment and program design. Similarly, to date research has not been conducted further elucidating factors *within the couple* that may be important in predicting participation in premarital prevention programs. This may be a fruitful endeavor to target and recruit those individuals who are most likely to need and benefit from the prevention efforts, especially in light of the expense and scarcity of clinical resources for prevention programs. As researchers develop and empirically examine theoretical models that comprehensively examine relationship distress and interpersonal violence, it is our hope that researchers continue to develop programs that are appropriate and beneficial, and that future research on recruitment identifies optimal strategies to encourage participation in such programs.

REFERENCES

Aiken, L. S., West, S. G., Woodward, C. K., Reno, R. R., and Reynolds, K. D. (1994). Increasing screening mammography in asymptomatic women: evaluation of a second-generation, theory-based program. *Health Psychology, 13,* 526-538.

Albee, G. W. (1990). The futility of psychotherapy. *Journal of Mind and Behavior, 11,* 369-384.

Avery-Leaf, S., Cascardi, M., O'Leary, D. K., and Cano, A. (1997). Efficacy of a dating violence prevention program on attitudes justifying aggression. *Journal of Adolescent Health, 21,* 11-17.

Bloom, B. L., Asher, S. J., and White, S. W. (1978). Marital disruption as a stressor: a review an analysis. *Psychological Bulletin, 85,* 867-894.

Bookwala, J., Frieze, I. H., Smith, C., and Ryan, K. (1992). Prediction of dating violence: A multivariate analysis. *Violence and Victims, 7,* 297-311.

Burman, B. and Margolin, G. (1992). Analysis of the association between marital relationships and health problems: an interactional perspective. *Psychological Bulletin, 112,* 39-63.

Cate, R. M., Henton, J. M., Koval, J., Christopher, F. S., and Lloyd, S. (1982). Premarital abuse: A social psychological perspective. *Journal of Family Issues, 3,* 79-90.

Christensen, A. and Heavey, C. L. (1999). Intervention for couples. *Annual Review of Psychology, 50,* 165-190.

Cornelius, T. L., Sullivan, K. T., Resseguie, N., and Milliken, J. (in press). Participation in prevention programs for dating violence: Beliefs about relationship violence and intention to participate. *Journal of Interpersonal Violence.*

Doss, B. D., Atkins, D. C. and Christensen, A. (2003). Who's dragging their feet? Husbands and wives seeking marital therapy. *Journal of Marital and Family Therapy 29,* 165-177.

Duncan, S. F., and Wood, M. M. (2003). Perceptions of marriage preparation among college-educated young adults with greater family-related risks for marital disruption. *The Family Journal: Counseling and Therapy for Couples and Families, 11,* 342-352.

Eisen, M., and Zellman, G. L. (1986). The role of health belief attitudes, sex education, and demographics in predicting adolescents' sexuality knowledge. *Health Education Quarterly, 13,* 9-22.

Fishbein, M., and Ajzen, I. (1975). *Belief, attitude, intention, and behavior : An introduction to theory and research.* Reading, Mass.: Addison-Wesley Pub. Co.

Foshee, V. A., Bauman, K. E., Arriaga, X. B., Helms, R. W., Koch, G. G., and Linder, G. F. (1998). An evaluation of safe dates, an adolescents dating violence prevention program. *American Journal of Public Health, 88,* 45-50.

Foshee, V. A., Bauman, K. E., Ennett, S. T., Linder, G. F., Benefield, T., and Suchindran, C. (2004). Assessing the long-term effects of the safe dates program and a booster in preventing and reducing adolescent dating violence victimization and perpetration. *American Journal of Public Health, 94,* 619-624.

Foshee, V. A., Bauman, K. E., Ennett, S. T., Suchindran, C., Benefield, T., & Linder, G. F. (2005). Assessing the effects of the dating violence prevention program "safe dates" using random coefficient regression modeling. *Prevention Science, 6,* 245-258.

Foshee, V. A., Bauman, K. E., and Greene, W. F. (2000). The safe dates program: 1-year follow-up results. *American Journal of Public Health, 90*, 1619-1622.

Foshee, V. A., Linder, G. F., Bauman, K. E., Langwick, S. A., Arriaga, X. B., Heath, J. L., McMahon, P. M., and Bangdiwala, S. (1996). The safe dates project: theoretical basis, evaluation design, and selected baseline findings. *American Journal of Preventive Medicine, 12*, 39-47.

Frieze, I. H. (2000). Violence in close relationships--development of a research area: comment on Archer (2000). *Psychological Bulletin, 126*, 681-684.

Gottman, J. M., and Notarius, C. I. (2000). Decade review: observing marital interaction. *Journal of Marriage and the Family, 62*, 927-947.

Gray, H. M., and Foshee, V. (1997). Adolescent dating violence: Differences between one-sided and mutually violent profiles. *Journal of Interpersonal Violence, 12*, 126-141.

Griffing, S., Ragin, F. D., Sage, R. E., Madry, L., Bingham, L. E., and Primm, B. J. (2002). Domestic violence survivors' self-identified reasons for returning to abusive relationships. *Journal of Interpersonal Violence, 17*, 306-319.

Guerney, L. (1977). A description and evaluation of a skills training program for foster parents. *American Journal of Community Psychology, 5*, 361-371.

Halford, W. K., O'Donnell, C., Lizzio, A., and Wilson, K. L. (2006). Do couples at high risk of relationship problems attend premarital education? *Journal of Family Psychology, 20*, 160-163.

Holmbeck, G. N. (1997). Toward terminological, conceptual, and statistical clarity in the study of mediators and moderators: Examples from the child-clinical and pediatric psychology literatures. *Journal of Consulting and Clinical Psychology, 65*, 599-610.

Hyman, R. B., and Baker, S. (1992). Construction of the Hyman-Baker mammography questionnaire, a measure of Health Belief Model variables. *Psychological Reports, 71*, 1203-1215.

Ingram, E. M. (2007). A comparison of help seeking between Latino and Non-Latino victims of intimate partner violence. *Violence and Victims, 13*, 159-171.

Jackson, S. M., Cram, F., and Seymour, F. W. (2000). Violence and sexual coercion in high school students' dating relationships. *Journal of Family Violence, 15*, 23-36.

Jacobson, N. S., and Gurman, A. S. (1995). *Clinical handbook of couple therapy.* New York, NY: Guilford Press.

Jette, A. M., Cummings, M., Brock, B. M., Phelps, M. C., and Naessens, J. (1981). The structure and reliability of health belief indices. *Health Services Research, 16*, 80-98.

Jezl, D. R., Molidor, C. E., and Wright, T. L. (1996). Physical, sexual and psychological abuse in high school dating relationships: Prevalence rates and self-esteem issues. *Child and Adolescent Social Work*, 13, 69-87.

Karney, B. R., and Bradbury, T. N. (1995). The longitudinal course of marital quality and stability: A review of theory, method, and research. *Psychological Bulletin, 118*, 3-34.

Katz, B. (1988). *How to market professional services.* New York: Nichols Publishing.

Kelly, E. L., and Conley, J. J. (1987). Personality and compatibility: A prospective analysis of marital stability and marital satisfaction. *Journal of Personality and Social Psychology, 5(2)*, 228-237.

Larson, J. H., and Holman, T. B. (1994). Premarital predictors of marital quality and stability, *Family Relations, 43*, 228-237.

Markman, H. J., Renick, M. J., Floyd, F. J., Stanley, S. M., and Clements, M. (1993). Preventing marital distress through communication and conflict management training: a 4- and 5-year follow-up. *Journal of Consulting and Clinical Psychology, 61,* 70-77.

Markman, H. J., Stanley, S. M., and Blumberg, S. L. (1994). *Fighting for your marriage: positive steps for preventing divorce and preserving a lasting love.* San Francisco, CA: Jossey-Bass.

Markman, H. J., Stanley, S. M., Jenkins, N. H., Petrella, J. N., and Wadsworth, M. E. (2006). Preventive Education: Distinctives and Directions. *Journal of Cognitive Psychotherapy, 20,* 411-433.

Morgan, D. L., and Scannell, A. U. (1998). *Planning focus groups.* Thousand Oaks, CA: Sage.

Morrison, D. M., Baker, S. A., and Gillmore, M. R. (2000). Using the theory of reasoned action to predict condom use among high risk heterosexual teens. In R. Norman and C. Abraham (Eds.), *Understanding and changing health behaviour: From health beliefs to self-regulation* (pp. 73-98). Amsterdam: Harwood Academic Publishers.

Nightingale, H., and Morrissette, P. (1993). Dating violence: attitudes, myths, and preventive programs. *Social Work in Education, 15,* 225-232.

O'Leary, D. K., Barling, J., Arias, I., Rosenbaum, A., Malone, J., and Tyree, A. (1989). Prevalence and stability of physical aggression between spouses: a longitudinal analysis. *Journal of Consulting and Clinical Psychology, 57,* 263-268.

Powell, G. S., and Wampler, K. S. (1982). Marriage enrichment participants: levels of marital satisfaction. *Family Relations, 31,* 389-393.

Prospero, M. (2006). The role of perceptions in dating violence among young adolescents. *Journal of Interpersonal Violence, 21,* 470-484.

Ronis, D. L., and Harel, Y. (1989). Health beliefs and breast examination behaviors: analyses of linear structural relations. *Psychology and Health, 34,* 259-285.

Rosenstock, I. M. (1966). Why people use health services. *Milbank Memorial Fund Quarterly, 44,* 94-124.

Schmoldt, R. A., Pope, C. R., and Hibbard, J. H. (1989). Marital interaction and the health and well-being of spouses. *Women and Health, 15,* 35-56.

Shadish, W. R., and Baldwin, S. A. (2005). Effects of behavioral marital therapy: a meta-analysis of randomized controlled trials. *Journal of Consulting and Clinical Psychology, 73,* 6-14.

Shurmann, L. A., and Rodriguez, C. M. (2006). Cognitive-affective predictors of women's readiness to end domestic violence relationships. *Journal of Interpersonal Violence, 21,* 1417-1439.

Silliman, B., and Schumm, W. R. (1995). Client interests in premarital counseling: A further analysis. *Journal of Sex and Marital Therapy, 21,* 43-56.

Silliman, B., Schumm, W. R., and Jurich, A. P. (1992). Young adults' preferences for premarital preparation program designs: An exploratory study. *Contemporary Family Therapy, 14,* 89-100.

Smith, D. M., and Donnelly, J. (2001). Adolescent dating violence: a multi-systemic approach of enhancing awareness in educators, parents, and society. *Journal of Prevention and Intervention in the Community, 21,* 53-64.

Stanley, S. M., Amato, P. R., Johnson, C. A., and Markman, H. J. (2006). Premarital education, marital quality, and marital stability: Findings from a large, random household survey. *Journal of Family Psychology, 20,* 117-126.

Straus, M. A., Hamby, S. L., Boney-McCoy, S., and Sugarman, D. B. (1996). The revised Conflict Tactics Scale (CTS2): Development and preliminary psychometric data. *Journal of Family Issues, 17,* 283-316.

Strecher, V. J., Champion, V. L., and Rosenstock, I. M. (1997). *The health belief model and health behavior.* New York, NY: Plenum Press.

Strube, M. J. (1988). The decision to leave an abusive relationship: empirical evidence and theoretical issues. *Psychological Bulletin, 104,* 236-250.

Sullivan, K. T., and Anderson, C. (2002). Recruitment of engaged couples for premarital counseling" An empirical examination of the importance of program characteristics and topics to potential participants. *The Family Journal: Counseling and Therapy for Couples and Families, 10,* 388-397.

Sullivan, K. T. and Bradbury, T. N. (1997). Are premarital prevention programs reaching couples at risk for marital dysfunction? *Journal of Consulting and Clinical Psychology, 65,* 24-30.

Sullivan, K. T., Pasch, L. A., Cornelius, T. L., and Cirigliano, E. (2004). Predicting participation in premarital prevention programs: The Health Belief Model and social norms. *Family Process, 43,* 175-194.

Truman-Schram, D.M., Cann, A., Calhoun, L., and Vanwallendael, L. (2000). Leaving an abusive dating relationship: an investment model comparison of women who stay versus women who leave. *Journal of Social and Clinical Psychology, 19,* 161-183.

VanWidenfelt, B., Markman, H. J., Guerney, B., Behrens, B. C., and Hosman, C. (1997). Prevention of relationship problems. In W. K. Halford and H. J. Markman (eds.), *Clinical handbook of marriage and couples interventions* (pp. 651-675). New York: Wiley.

Whitaker, D. J., Morrison, S., Lindquist, S., Hawkins, S. R., O'Neil, J. A., Nesius, A. M., Mathew, A., and Reese, L. (2006). A critical review of interventions for the primary prevention of perpetration of partner violence. *Aggression and Violent Behavior, 11,* 151-166.

In: Psychological Counseling Research Focus
Editors: James A. Patterson et al, pp. 23-45

ISBN 978-1-60456-041-1
© 2008 Nova Science Publishers, Inc.

Chapter 2

THE EFFECTS OF A PSYCHO-EDUCATIONAL GROUP INTERVENTION ON THE QUALITY OF LIFE OF YOUNG WOMEN WITH BREAST CANCER

Joan R. Bloom[1], Susan L. Stewart[2], Carol D'Onofrio[1], Judith Luce[2], Priscilla Banks[3], Pat Fobair[4], and Merrilee Morrow[3]

[1]University of California, Berkeley, CA, USA
[2]University of California, San Francisco, CA, USA
[3]Northern California Cancer Center, Fremont, CA, USA
[4]Stanford University, CA, USA

ABSTRACT

Objective

To assess the outcomes of a psycho-educational group intervention on the physical, mental, and social well-being of young women treated for breast cancer.

Background

Psycho-educational group interventions are evidence-based and focus on providing skills in coping, problem solving, and communication as well as information regarding cancer and its treatment. Our approach was refined from information derived through focus groups and interviews with a similar group of 336 women.

Method

Young women (age 50 or less) were identified through the Rapid Case Ascertainment of the SEER Cancer Registry of the Greater San Francisco Bay Area (n=363). An experimental design with random assignment was used. The experimental condition was composed of 25 multi-ethnic groups, average size of 7.4 women that met for 10 weekly two-hour sessions. Analysis used a "Difference of a Difference model." Using an "intent to treat" approach, change was assessed between pre-post test and pre-6 months. Outcome measures were psychological and physical well-being. In addition to main effects, interactions with race/ethnicity, time since diagnosis, emotional support and previous counseling were included in the models.

Results

No main effects on psychological or physical measures of well-being were found for pre to post-test, albeit 88% of the experimental group found the intervention to be helpful. Interactions were found for positive effects of the intervention for women, who reported poorer emotional support, were a longer time since diagnosis (adjuvant therapy completed, except for tamoxifen), and who had previous counseling.

Discussion

Initially, women agreed to be randomized prior to knowing the day and location of the group's meetings. This resulted in a large number of women who never attended a group (n=60). One reason, the group intervention may not have been effective was that invidious comparisons between women in the group were made based on stage of disease and "downward comparisons" were not helpful (Helgeson, 1999). Alternatively, the support provided by "similar others" may have been less helpful (Thoits, 1995). There is some evidence that intervention may have been too short to develop skills to resolve problems (those with prior counseling did better). Higher levels of mood dysphoria may have been due to the difficulties with maintaining denial (Bloom, 1978). Findings from this study are consistent with those of Helgeson, 1999 and Antoni et al. 2001 whose populations and psychological intervention differed. Our findings from subgroup analyses suggest that women who were emotionally needy benefited more from groups' psychological support.

Implications

Screen women for low social support and previous counseling and refer to group interventions. Hold groups at the end of treatment when they may be better prepared to take advantage of the skills training. Finally, a longer series or a second series of sessions may be needed.

INTRODUCTION

Background

Breast cancer is the most common cancer among US women in every major racial/ethnic group. Currently, about 26 percent of all newly diagnosed invasive cancers are of the breast (Ries et al., 2007). Of this number, 23 percent are in women under 50 (Smigal et al., 2006). As evidence accumulated suggesting that both medical and psychosocial issues were different for this group of women compared to older women, younger women became the focus of a special conference put on by the National Cancer Institute and subsequently a programmatic focus for research (Bloom and Kessler, 1994). Some of the special issues and concerns of younger women are:

- While there is consensus on screening recommendations for post-menopausal women, mammography screening is still controversial for women under 50 (Qaseem et al., 2007).
- Mammography is less effective in younger women who are more likely to have dense breast tissue; thus, it is less likely to detect tumors and tumors may be detected by a clinical breast exam or by the women herself when the tumor is larger (Qaseem et al. 2007)
- Further, both incidence rates (0.3% per year) and mortality rates (2.2% per year) for younger women have declined over the past two decades (Ries et al., 2007).
- Breast tumors in younger women tend to be more aggressive, often requiring multi-modal treatments, which can have side-effects. (Shapiro and Recht, 1994; Osteen et al., 1993; Quivey et al., 1998).
- Women who receive chemotherapy and are between 40 and 50 are likely to have abrupt and permanent menopause.
- There is evidence that past systematic adjuvant treatment is associated with poorer quality of life as the time post diagnosis increases (Ganz, 2002).
- The combination of decreasing incidence (albeit slowly) and mortality rates means that more young women are becoming long-term survivors. Indeed, the 5-year relative survival rate in U.S. women under age 50 has risen from 76.7% for those diagnosed in 1975-1977 to 87.3% for women diagnosed with breast cancer in 1996-2003 (Ries et al., 2007). This increase in survival has occurred in all racial/ethnic groups and is attributed to greater utilization of breast cancer screening and improvements in treatment (Smigal et al., 2006).

For the reasons cited above as well as their life circumstances, younger women with breast cancer may face different problems then post-menopausal women. Most are married, employed, and often still have young children at home. Research findings indicate that younger women are at increased risk for psychological and social problems (Bloom and Kessler, 1994). These effects may be compounded for women who are divorced, have young children, or who are economically disadvantaged. There is also evidence that the burdens of the diagnosis and treatment may fall heavier on women who are from culturally and ethnically diverse backgrounds (Bloom and Kessler, 1994). Thus, their need for information about their disease, its treatment, and consequences as well as support from others may be provided by appropriately planned and timed interventions.

The objective of the current study was to design and assess an educational and support intervention that would ameliorate the psychosocial effects of the breast cancer diagnosis/ treatment, thus preparing the women for the future.

Interventions for improving well-being following a diagnosis of breast cancer generally focus on either education or emotional support. These interventions can be offered individually or in group settings. The latter has become more prevalent due to cost considerations. Several interventions to be described below contain both an educational/informational component in addition to emotional support.

Support Groups as Interventions for Newly Diagnosed Women

Currently, the most common resource for women following initial cancer treatment are peer and professionally led support groups (Bloom, Ross, Burnell, 1978; Bloom, 1986). Professionally led support groups are ubiquitous and found in hospital as well as community settings (Spiegel, Bloom and Yalom, 1986). Group therapy, as designed and popularized by Irvin Yalom, MD of Stanford University, was adapted for women with breast cancer at the request and encouragement of a woman with metastatic breast cancer. Twenty-five years later, 11 randomized clinical trials (RCT) were found in the literature; only a few focused on women newly diagnosed with breast cancer and many of them were published before the turn of the century (Gottlieb and Wachala, 2007).

The seminal and, perhaps most controversial RCT, was designed to assess the effects of a therapeutically designed support group intervention on the psychological and physical well-being of women with metastatic cancer. Women were randomly assigned to a group (one of three) or to the control condition (usual care). A psychiatrist and a co-leader ran groups. Sessions lasted for 90 minutes and used "supportive-expressive" group therapy, which provides mutual support and opportunities for emotional expression and confrontation of existential challenges to facilitate coping. In addition to the group session, training for self-hypnosis for pain control was offered and family members, if willing, were invited to attend the group sessions every six weeks. Reductions in mood dysphoria, improvements in adaptive coping, and reductions in pain were found as a function of the group experience (Spiegel, Bloom and Yalom, 1981; Spiegel and Bloom, 1983) and extensions in length of life were observed (Spiegel et al, 1989). While a number of attempts to replicate the findings have taken place, they have been only partially successful. They have replicated findings related to quality of life, but not length of life (Goodwin et al., 2001; Kissane et al, 2004).

A second therapeutic approach used in support groups is cognitive behavioral therapy. Its approach is to train participants to modify their behavior or cognitions by the active acquisition of specific coping skills (Edmonds, Lockwood, and Cunningham, 1999; Simpson et al, 2002; Telch and Telch, 1986). Among 22 studies of cognitive behavioral stress management reviewed by Trijsburg and colleagues (1992), the reduction of stress and distress were the primary goals of the therapy. About half had additional goals including preserving social support, opportunities to express feelings, encouraging hope, positive self-image and social well-being. A ten-week study RCT of 100 women following their diagnosis of early stage breast cancer is characteristic of this approach (Antoni et al, 2001). The goal of the intervention was to teach behavioral and cognitive strategies and give the women the opportunity to role-play the strategies in a supportive group setting. At post-test the intervention reduced the prevalence of moderate depression, but it did not reduce other measures of emotional distress. It did increase the optimism of the women and their reports that having breast cancer had made positive contributions to their lives (benefit finding). These findings held at three months post-test as well. Upon further analysis, the intervention was found to have the most effect on women who were the least optimistic and least likely to report benefit finding (Antoni et al, 2001).

A third more general approach, combines education, either on the disease, cancer treatment, procedural issues, and/or education, with group support. An early study of this approach included groups organized by Telch and Telch (1986) in a three arm RCT that compared group coping skills instruction, supportive group therapy, and a no-treatment control in 41 persons of different genders and cancers. Another is the RCT carried out by Jacobs and her colleagues (1983) of a cancer information pamphlet designed for persons with Hodgkin's disease who were assigned to one of four interventions, combining education with group support. In the former study, persons assigned to the coping skills groups demonstrated improvements in mood, coping, physical and work related activities, and intimacy, while those assigned to peer support showed little improvement in mood and the controls' mood deteriorated. In the latter study, while the participants liked the support groups, improvements in psychological parameters and knowledge were equally likely to be found in the education only group.

The most important study combining education and support is by Helgeson and her colleagues (1999), who used a similar design, peer group support with and without an educational component, a classroom type education intervention and a usual care control. Peer discussion consisted of a one-hour peer support discussion and a 45-minute formal educational component; topics included an overview of breast cancer, side effects of treatment, nutrition, exercise, body image, and future health issues. A nurse and a social worker led the 28 groups of 8-12 women. In addition to eight weekly sessions, there were three booster sessions. The pre-post test design also contained follow-up assessments at six months and, again, at three years. Consistent with the findings of Jacobs et al. (1983), Helgeson and her colleagues (1999) found positive effects on all outcomes (self-esteem, positive affect, reduced negative affect, body image, perceived self-control, and health related quality of life) for the education component. Weaker findings were found for the groups that combined education and peer support, while the findings were negative for those in the peer support groups. One explanation for this negative finding is that the women made invidious comparisons depending on the number of positive lymph nodes each woman had. The number of positive lymph nodes became the basis of the status order within the groups as well as their seating arrangement. The positive findings lasted for three years but then started to decrease (Helgeson et al., 2001).

In summary, the support group literature demonstrates that different theoretical approaches to providing support group interventions to people following the diagnosis of cancer, in general, and breast cancer, in particular, can be effective in reducing distress. However, for newly diagnosed women, the findings suggest that support groups do not benefit women on average, rather they do benefit subgroups of women. This literature, however, does not answer questions about who is at risk for mood distress and what is the best timing for intervention. The one study that provides some guidelines for researchers and practitioners is the Helgeson (1999) study that suggests guidelines for group composition, i.e. group members should be similar in terms of the stage of their disease.

What was the best timing for the intervention? Crisis therapists advocate early intervention as the cancer diagnosis creates disequilibria. During this time, help is more likely to be accepted. In addition, the individual can be influenced to choose healthy coping responses (Caplan, 1964). Research in psycho-oncology, on the other hand, has found that mood, while slowly improving following a breast cancer diagnosis, dips around one year post-diagnosis. This dip, coinciding with the end of bio-medical therapy, suggests that the women's reduction in medical support results in feelings of abandonment following the end of treatment. Thus, the end of treatment is a natural time to provide intervention (PABC, 1987; Bloom and Kessler, 1994).

Who is most likely to benefit from intervention? Approximately 25% of newly diagnosed cancer patients report significant levels of depression and anxiety. Initial levels of mood distress are strong predictors of subsequent distress (Ell et al., 1989). Other predictors are a history of depression, low self-esteem, external locus of control, and neuroticism. Women who have other health problems, are divorced, or have low social support are also at greater risk for psychosocial and adjustment problems following treatment for breast cancer (Ganz 1988; Ganz et al, 1996; Bloom and Kessler, 1994). Finally women who have upper body disability due to cancer treatment should improve as a result of exercise to improve upper body strength and range of motion (Gaskin et al., 1989; Satariano, et al., 1990).

Should intervention be ethnic specific? The mental health literature indicates that in the therapeutic relationship, matching of race/ethnicity improves the relationship (Flaskerud, 1990). Bringing women together who have a common concern will assist in bonding. Whether the common diagnosis overrides the importance of ethnic matching is unclear. This is one of the foci of Phase I of the currently reported study.

Objective

The major objective of this study was to address the psychosocial and educational needs of ethnically and culturally diverse women living in the San Francisco Bay Area through a group intervention that provided both peer support and met the educational needs of the women. To implement this objective, the study was designed in two phases.

The aims of the first phase were: 1) To assess the level of psychosocial distress, concerns regarding body image and sexuality, functional adaptation, and type of medical treatment of women diagnosed with breast cancer at age 50 or younger, and 2) To describe differences among this population-based cohort by their culture and ethnicity, the type of medical treatment received, and factors that affect the timing of their response (such as a delay in psychosocial distress due to type of treatment received or cultural factors). To gather this information, multiple methods were used. First, a descriptive survey of 336 women was completed. This was followed by conducting five ethnic specific focus groups composed of women who participated in the survey. The findings of this assessment were used to specify the design and content of a ten-week education and support intervention, which was conducted during the second phase of the study.

The aim of this second phase was to design, implement, and evaluate the effectiveness of providing a culturally sensitive education and peer support intervention within seven months of the women's diagnosis of breast cancer. The effectiveness of the intervention was assessed by the following: 1) the level of psychosocial distress was expected to be reduced; 2) the woman's self-image including sexuality was expected to improve; 3) the woman's physical functioning was expected to improve more in the intervention group than in the control group. The effectiveness of the intervention was assessed using a pre-post test design with a follow-up survey completed six months after the pre-test.

Methodology and Findings for Phase I

The first phase of the study was designed to assess the characteristics of women who were most at the risk for mood distress, the timing of the intervention to coincide with the time post diagnosis when women would benefit most from intervention and the ethnic composition of the peer support groups. A survey was designed to focus on the first two issues--to assess the needs of young women with breast cancer by determining the type of problems they had and to determine the optimal timing of the intervention, that is, whether their problems and needs were greater close to diagnosis or at the end of treatment. The survey was designed so that equal numbers of women were assessed soon after diagnosis (within two months) and further from diagnosis (6-7 months following diagnosis). The instrument was designed to assess the frequency of the different physical, psychological, and social problems these women reported. To gather information regarding the third issue, six ethnic specific focus groups were conducted.

Sample for Needs Assessment Survey. The Rapid Case Ascertainment system of the Northern California Cancer Center's (NCCC) identified by the Greater Bay Area Cancer Registry, which is part of the Surveillance, Epidemiology and End Results (SEER) program and the California Cancer Registry, collected all cases of breast cancer in women age 50 and under reported during the period of October 1994 to April 1995 (for the main part of the study, Phase II, cases were collected through 1997). Following accepted procedure, 1) the physicians of each case were contacted, 2) following physician assent, a letter was sent to the woman, 3) the interviewer contacted the woman by phone and if she agreed, an appointment was made for the in-person interview. The sample consisted of 336 women (80% of eligible cases who were reached). Half of these women were interviewed within two months of treatment and the other half were interviewed 6-7 months following diagnosis. An additional 29 women participated in pilot interviews. All women were interviewed in English.

Socio-demographic characteristics of the sample indicate that the women were young and well educated (50% were less than age 45, 50% were college graduates and only 3% did not graduate from high school). Most worked (59% full time and 18% part-time); were married (65%) and had children (63%); and were Euro-American (71%). We had expected a majority to have a lumpectomy and were surprised to find that 46% had a lumpectomy, 47% had a single mastectomy, 3% had a double mastectomy, and 4% had no surgical treatment at the time of the interview (Bloom et al., 1998).

Measurement

The interview instruments contained general measures of health status, measures of adjustment to illness, information about how the women's breast cancer was detected and her knowledge of the treatment and preferences for making treatment decisions, socio-demographic characteristics, including measures of work history, health insurance, family composition and family relationships. The following measures were collected for both phases of the study:

Psychological dysphoria was measured by the Center for Epidemiological Studies-Depression Scale (CES-D) as it is a population-based measure (Radloff, 1977). To reduce the length of the survey, a shortened version of this scale was used (Kohout et al., 1993) for Phase I but not for Phase II.

Self-Esteem was measured using Rosenberg's (1965) scale; it contains ten Likert formatted items, which were added together following the procedure suggested by Lewis (1989).

Health Related Quality of Life was measured using the MOS SF 36 (Ware and Sherbourne, 1992). This scale measures eight different health concepts: physical functioning (PF), role limitations due to physical problems (RP), bodily pain (BP), general health (GH), vitality (energy/fatigue) (VT), social functioning (SF), role limitations due to emotional problems (RE), mental health (MH). Five scales define health status as the absence of limitation or disability (PF, RP, BP, SF, and RE). The data were scored using the RAND method. The highest possible score is 100 when no limitations or disabilities are observed. For the other three scales, (GH, VT, and MH) which are "bipolar" and measure a much wider range of positive and negative health states, a score in the mid-range is based on respondents report of no limitations or disability. Higher scores (closer to 100) mean that respondents have reported positive states and evaluate their health favorably.

These generic measures were supplemented with several cancer specific measures. The intrusiveness of breast cancer and its treatment into other life domains was measured using the Intrusiveness of Treatment Scale (Devins, 1994). The women's cancer related concerns were measured by the Problem scale developed by Schain (1979). This scale contains 23 Likert scaled items. The Cronbach's alpha for the scale is 0.85. Three factor derived subscales were developed from the Problem scale: Patient-physician communication, self-image, and future concerns (Worry about the Future). The Symptom Concerns scale measured symptom distress due to breast cancer treatment, seven items that measure treatment related symptoms, five menopausal symptoms, and two chemotherapy-related side effects (nausea and hair loss). We chose to keep these scales separate even though they were sufficiently inter-correlated to be combined. A specific measure of cancer related fatigue was also measured by a single item that is highly correlated with the Vitality Scale (VT) of the Health Related Quality of Life measure described above ($r=-0.61$).

As described above socio-demographic characteristics were collected, including age, education, marital status, family composition, and work status. In addition, information regarding their medical treatment was collected. For this study, we were particularly interested in 1) the time post-diagnosis - either less than 2 months or 6-7 months, 2) the type of treatment they received - lumpectomy or mastectomy (single or double), and 3) whether they were currently receiving adjuvant treatment or not (either completed treatment or had not started it). The type of treatment, radiation therapy, chemotherapy, or tamoxifen, was also collected. Stage of disease at time of diagnosis was collected from the cancer registry files at the NCCC.

Analytic Strategy for Needs Assessment Survey

Bivariate analyses were carried out that compared the sample of women on three parameters: time post diagnosis -1-2 months compared to 6-7 months; type of surgical treatment received--mastectomy compared to breast conserving surgery; and whether the women was currently receiving adjuvant treatment or not.

Results of the Needs Assessment Survey

Emotional Distress and Time from Diagnosis

Women with breast cancer were compared on the eight subscales of the SF 36 based on their time post-diagnosis, the type of surgical treatment, and whether they were currently receiving cancer treatment. Women further from diagnosis were significantly more likely to report fewer limitations due to bodily pain ($p=.03$), but were more likely to rate their general health (GH) as lower ($p=.04$). Women further from diagnosis reported significantly more problems with self-image than did the newly diagnosed ($p=0.02$). However, there were no differences between time post-treatment and measures of mood dysphoria including depression.

When type of treatment was compared, women having a mastectomy rated their health lower than women who had breast-conserving treatment ($p=0.02$) and reported poor self-image ($p=0.0001$) and more treatment related fatigue ($p=0.05$) than the women who had breast-conserving treatment.

Women who were in treatment reported significantly greater limitations on five of the scales: bodily pain ($p=0.01$), vitality ($p=0.02$), social functioning ($p=0.008$) and role limitations due to physical functioning ($p=0.005$) and emotions ($p=0.006$). Women who were in treatment also reported greater treatment related fatigue ($p=0.0001$), more depression ($p=0.005$), and intrusiveness of treatment into other domains of their life ($p=0.0004$). In other words, many of the differences between the women were due to the type of treatment they received as well as whether they were still in active treatment. While these findings were related to time post-diagnosis, type of treatment and being on-treatment were more important predictors of differences between the women.

Ethnic Specific Focus Groups

Following the survey, five ethnic specific focus groups (30 women total) were composed: an African American, a Latina, and a Chinese focus group each with six participants; a Filipino focus group with five participants; and a Euro-American focus group with seven participants. Twenty-five out of the thirty participants were recruited from the sample of women who completed the assessment interviews. Five additional women were recruited to increase focus group participation from women from Chinese (n=3) and Filipina (n=2) backgrounds. All groups were held in early evening; participants were provided transportation if needed, a light dinner, and a small honorarium.

The moderator in each of the groups was of the same racial/ethnic background as the participants. In the cases of the Latina, Chinese, and Filipina groups, she was also bilingual. Also present at each of the focus groups were an observer who took notes and operated the tape recorder and a member of the intervention development team. All groups lasted about two hours and used the same moderator's guide, although group process determined to some extent how detailed the discussion were on any given issue.

Analytic Strategy for Focus Groups

The transcripts of each focus group were first reviewed individually and broad themes were coded. From the themes, more detailed coding categories were developed. Each transcript was coded by two persons (in most cases one of the coders had also been a group moderator). The coded data were transferred onto a grid to systematically compare data from the five groups. Finally one coder summarized the data and the findings corroborated by the others (Somkin et al., unpublished).

Focus Group Findings

Experiences with support groups. While women in all groups reported having received considerable emotional support during the diagnosis and treatment of their breast cancer, the women of color reported less exposure to support in a formal group. They also expressed reluctance to talk in a group setting.

Benefits and barriers of education/support group experience. Two main benefits were reported by all groups: 1) Obtaining emotional support and information. Latinas and Euro-Americans mentioned that they wanted to attend a group to be able to talk to others who had "been there" and that attending a group would help them know that they were not alone. Filipinas also mentioned the need to bond with women who had similar concerns, and African Americans mentioned the benefit of sharing with others, especially if there was no family support. Chinese women perceived the group process as a way to empower themselves and to help them accept and deal with the fact that they had breast cancer. 2) Most women shared three negative features of focus groups: distaste for complaining, fear of disclosure, and fear of facing women with more advanced cancer.

Multi-ethnic versus ethnic-specific focus. An underlying question was the extent to which the experience of coping with breast cancer was a universal experience, one that transcends cultural differences. While there was variation in the extent of personal experience with formal support groups, there was surprising similarity in their views about the potential benefits of attending a support group, the characteristics of groups, and group process that they favored. In all of the groups, the women expressed a desire to come together to share experiences and practical tips with other women with breast cancer and also a reluctance to come together to complain about their situation. They were uniformly afraid of facing women who had undergone recurrences of their cancer. The fact that women of color generally expressed less comfort than Euro-American women participating in formal groups, and particularly in disclosing their feelings, could represent either a fundamentally different approach to obtaining emotional support among women of color compared to Euro-American women (a real "cultural difference") or it could simply be a reflection of a specific time in our history that may be changing (acculturation) (Somkin et al., unpublished manuscript).

Discussion and Conclusions

A workshop of the key staff and consultants was held to discuss the findings of the needs assessment and to answer the three questions felt to be important in planning the education/support intervention. After the data from the transcripts were analyzed, they were presented to the groups along with the completed analyses. The implicit assumption of the need for an educational group support intervention was validated by the discussion of the women who attended the focus groups. Responses to the three questions follow:

When is the best time for an intervention? We expected to find that the young women would experience more problems at one time period versus the other (one-two months following diagnosis compared to six-seven months following diagnosis, usually at the end of treatment). Instead, we found that there weren't fewer problems at one time versus the second time, but that the women's problems were different. Further, differences were as likely to be related to the type of treatment and whether the women were on active treatment than just time post-diagnosis. Therefore, the decision, strongly advocated by our team's medical oncologist, was made to include women any time along the continuum from diagnosis until the seven months following diagnosis.

Who is most likely to benefit from intervention? The findings of the analyses suggest that women who perceived themselves to be lacking in a support system, had more difficulties following treatment (usually due to having a mastectomy and/or chemotherapy), were still in treatment, and women of color, especially those who were poor, were expected to benefit most from the intervention. While it was decided to invite all women into the intervention, specific assistance with transportation and child care seemed to be ways of assisting women to attend who might be most likely to benefit from the intervention.

Should intervention be ethnic specific? The findings from the focus groups that the commonality of having breast cancer was more important than being in an ethnic specific support group facilitated the decision to have multi-ethnic groups. However, concern was expressed regarding women of color feeling isolated. To reduce this concern multi-ethnic leaders were recruited and trained. Groups were composed keeping in mind both geography and the ethnic distribution of the women in the region. If, for example, only one African American woman was randomized to the group, then one of the leaders in the group would also be African-American. If their two African American women randomized to a group, then the leaders could be of other ethnicities.

PHASE II

Methods

Psycho-Educational Support Group Intervention

The intervention occurred over ten weeks. Each session took place over two hours and focused on educational topics or coping skills. Seven of the sessions were common across the groups; three, including a special group for spouse/partners, were tailored to the interests of the group's members. Two leaders led the multi-ethnic groups. Session objectives and topics are displayed in Figure 1. A detailed discussion of the intervention and the process evaluation that was completed were reported elsewhere (Bloom et al., 1999).

Training of Leaders. Prior to beginning the intervention, 12 women were recruited and trained to lead the psycho-educational intervention. The women were multi-ethnic--five were Euro-American, three were Asian, three were African American, and one was Hispanic. Four were bilingual (Spanish and Chinese) albeit the women in the intervention all spoke English. Most of the leaders/facilitators were between 30 and 44, two were over 45 and one was under 30. Three were breast cancer survivors. Their professional background also varied (three were social workers, three were counselors, one was a registered nurse, two were ministers, and three were community workers). All had experience working with cancer patients.

Session	Topics	Objectives
1	Impact of Cancer*	Develop Group Adhesiveness Share Personal Feelings
2	Identify Needs and Resources*	Identify Personal Needs Find Community Resources
3	Communication and Assertiveness*	Tell Medical Doctor What You Need Tell Family Members What You Need Tell People At Work What You Need
4	Managing Negative Feelings*	Identifying Negative Feelings Thinking Constructively Solving Problems
5	Healing My Inner Self	Improving Self-Image Improving Self-Esteem
6	Breast Self-Examination*	Learning BSE
7	Nutrition*	Improving Nutrition
8	Improving Relationships	With Spouse/Partner With Children Improve Sex Life
9	Pleasant Activities	Enjoy Pleasant Activities Relax
10	Planning for the Future*	Review Coping Strategies Develop A Personal Plan Bring Closure To Group

Figure 1. Topics in psycho-educational intervention.

The training of the group facilitators took place over several sessions, one eight-hour session and five four-hour sessions. A training manual was developed for their use under the leadership of one of the authors. In addition, the leaders attended a half-day monthly session with the training staff to discuss problems and issues, and the trainers attended group meetings on a regularly scheduled basis. The project coordinator attended the first three sessions of each group to ensure consistency of training. The trainers also attended at least one session of each group. After the ninth session, they also met with the two group leaders to discuss whether referrals to other services, including counseling, were needed for any of the group members.

Intervention Delivery. The groups meet weekly and were led by two facilitators. The experienced group facilitators were teamed with less experienced facilitators. As described above, the facilitators contributed to the ethnic diversity of the groups. To reduce the risk of non-attendance, women were invited to groups that were no further than 45 minutes driving time from their home. Assistance was given for both transportation and childcare. Locations for the groups were selected for convenience to public transportation, for safety, as the groups usually met in the late afternoon or early evening and for comfort. The groups met in a variety of locations throughout the San Francisco Bay Area. Meeting sites included hotels (most provided the rooms gratis), libraries, restaurants and non-profit agencies (since this was a community study, hospitals were excluded as meeting sites).

Process Evaluation. Prior to beginning the intervention, a pilot of the entire intervention was completed. Based on the experiences of the pilot group, modifications were made to the intervention materials and training of the leaders. After the sixth group of 25 was completed (all group facilitators had completed one group), efforts were made to incorporate feedback from participants and trainers in the monthly facilitators' meetings. Participants who had completed the intervention assessed each of the individual sessions, rating the entire intervention as well as what they considered to be the most important aspects of the interventions. Of the 100 women who participated in these initial groups, 75 completed the process evaluation questionnaires. Two of the sessions, participants negatively assessed Session Four- Community Resources and Session Seven-Nutrition, and efforts were directed to improve these sessions. The process evaluation indicates that these improvements were effective (Bloom et al., 1999).

Design of the Evaluation. An experimental design with random assignment was employed to assess this controlled field trial of the intervention. Women were randomly assigned to the intervention or control group following the initial interview. The outcome evaluation included assessment at three points--before the groups begin (pretest), at the end of the ten-week intervention (posttest), and three months following the intervention (follow-up).

Sample

The sample consisted of 363 women (50% response rate), who were identified from five of the counties covered through the SEER and California Cancer Tumor Registries in the San Francisco Bay Area (San Francisco, Alameda, Contra Costa, San Mateo and Santa Clara). In order to include as many minority women as possible, Marin County, which has a small minority population, was excluded from the sample. Of the 363 women, 185 were randomized to the Intervention Group and 178 to the Control Group. At first, women who agreed to participate were randomly assigned before they knew the location and meeting times for the group. This resulted in a large number of women who initially agreed to participate but could not. Based on the early experience, the procedure was changed so that only women who were willing and able to attend the intervention at its scheduled time and location were randomized.

Measurement

Data to evaluate the effectiveness of the intervention were collected by a structured in-person interview at pre-test. The post-test survey and follow-up survey were conducted by telephone.

Measures used as statistical controls include socio-demographic factors such as age, education, marital status, number of children and ethnicity. Disease/treatment factors include the type of surgical treatment and the type of adjuvant therapy and whether the women had positive lymph nodes. Two psychological factors were also included as control variables-- whether the women had received previous counseling either before or during the intervention period. In addition to group counseling, other types of counseling the women had received in the past were assessed. Second, a measure of emotional support was included. This is a 10 item scale developed by Flamer (unpublished), it has a Cronbach alpha of greater than 0.80.

Outcome measures included general measures of health status taken from Ware and Shelbourne's SF-36 from which the physical component and the mental component were calculated as well as a number of breast cancer specific measures (Ware an Sherborne, 1992). The specific measures included the women's coping response, worry about the future, doctor-patient relationship, self-image, sexuality and nutrition. A detailed description of the outcome measures was presented earlier. Measures not previously described are as follows: Mood distress was measured by the CES-D (Center for Epidemiological Studies-Depression Scale). It is a 20- item scale measuring depression and has been used in both clinical and in community samples of cancer patients. Coefficient alphas of 0.85 were found in the community sample and the test-retest reliability was 0.57 (Radloff, 1977). In contrast to Phase One where a shortened version was used, the entire scale was used in Phase Two. Nutrition was measured using Block's fruit and vegetable screener and fat screener (Block et al., 1990). Sexuality was measured using several questions drawn from the National Tamoxifen Study (Ganz et al., 1996). From Schain's problem concerns scale (1979) several factor-derived subscales were developed to measure doctor-patient communication, worry about the future, and self-image. Palliative coping was measured by four self-assessed habits utilized by the women to reduce emotional tension, including smoking too much, drinking too much alcohol, eating too much, taking drugs for pep or taking drugs to sleep or become calm. This measure has been used in other studies and predicts medical care utilization among college students as well as adjustment to cancer (Bloom and Spiegel, 1986; Bloom et al, 1998).

Analytic Strategy for the Intervention

To analyze these data, a "Difference of a Difference" model with multiple regression analysis was used. Change was assessed between pretest and posttest and between pretest and follow-up (three months following the posttest measure). Pretest values of the outcomes were included in each model to control for initial differences in outcome measures. Both intent to treat (all individuals randomized regardless of their attendance at the intervention) and intensity of the intervention (whether they attended 6 or more sessions of the intervention) were assessed simultaneously. Finally, in addition to the main effects, interactions with race/ethnicity, time since diagnosis, emotional support, and previous counseling were assessed. The latter were included as one of the initial questions in the study (see above) was to determine who was most likely to benefit from intervention.

RESULTS

Process Evaluation

At the end of the intervention, women were asked to assess the intervention. Overall, 87.3% of the women found the intervention to be "very helpful" or "somewhat helpful."

Only 5.7% of the women assessed the intervention as "not at all helpful." Two women attended only one session. Their behavior might have been due to their state of health or to their lack of enthusiasm about the intervention.

Main Effects

Pretest to Posttest. No main effects were found from pre- to post-test. That is, none of the outcome measures had a statistically significant intervention effect.

Pretest to Follow-up (three months following the intervention). Main effects were found for the mental health component of the SF-36 and for sexual problems. For the mental health component, the coefficient for six or more group sessions was –4.82 (S.E.=2.04) and for sexual problems the coefficient was 0.81 (S.E.=0.34). These results indicate that women in the intervention reported poorer mental health than those in the control condition and more sexual problems. These findings are inconsistent with our expectations.

Interactions

Pretest to Posttest

Interactions were found with emotional support, time since diagnosis, and previous counseling. No interactions were found for race/ethnicity (Table 2).

Emotional Support. Interactions with emotional support were found for the Total Problem Scales and its subscales (palliative coping, worry about the future and patient-physician communication) and symptom distress. The less emotional support reported, the more beneficial was the effect of the intervention on reducing palliative coping, reducing worry about the future, improving patient-physician communication and reducing symptoms of distress.

Time since diagnosis. Interactions were found for some of the SF-36 subscales (the physical component, physical role, and physical functioning) and for mood dysphoria as measured by the CES-D. The effect of receipt of the intervention on physical outcomes and mood was stronger among women further from diagnosis (albeit up to seven months from diagnosis), than among those closer to diagnosis.

Table 1. Sample Characteristics (n=363)

	Intervention (N=185) (Percent)	Control (N=178) (Percent)
Socio-Demographic		
Age under 45*	52	43
Race/Ethnicity		
White	71	71
African American	9	7
Hispanic	4	8
Asian	16	14
Marital Status (Married)	70	67
Education (College Graduate)	57	57
Occupation (Professional)	49	41
Working at Pre-Test	75	80
Health Insurance		
Public	3	3
Private	94	96
None	3	1
Number of Children* (at home)		
None	38	46
One	26	29
Two	36	25
Medical/Treatment		
Cancer in Family	81	83
Had Mastectomy*	62	51
Has Positive Nodes	36	34
Prognosis (Excellent/Good)	84	80
Counseling		
Psychological Counseling (Prior to intervention)	50	42
Other Counseling (During intervention)**		
Group	22	29
Individual/Psychologist	19	20
Individual/Social Worker	6	5
Other Counseling	4	5

* $p < .10$ (p-value)
** Multiple responses

Table 2. Results (Pre To Post-Test) Interactions

Effect	Coefficient	S.E.
Emotional Support		
Palliative Coping	0.06	0.03*
Worry About Future	0.08	0.03*
Patient-Physician Communication	0.10	0.04*
Total Problem Scale	0.30	0.11*
Symptom Distress	0.26	0.13
Previous Counseling		
Outlook on Life	3.91	1.52*
Time From Diagnosis		
SF-36-Physical Component	0.05	.02
SF-36-Physical Role	0.27	.12
SF-36-Physical Functioning	0.10	.05
CES-D	-0.06	.02

Previous Counseling. An interaction was found with one's outlook on life. The effect of receipt of the intervention on outlook on life was greater among women with previous counseling than among those without previous counseling.

Table 3. Results (Pre To 6 Months) Interactions

Effect	Coefficient	S.E.
Previous Counseling		
Self-Image	-.086	0.32*
Time Since Diagnosis		
SF-36 Emotional Role	0.22	0.11
Symptom Distress	0.02	0.01

Pretest to Follow-up

Interactions were found for time since diagnosis and for previous counseling. Interactions with emotional support and race/ethnicity were not found (Table 3).

Time since diagnosis. Interactions were found for SF-36 emotional role scale and for symptom distress. The intervention had a more beneficial effect on one's emotional well-being interfering less with carrying out their social roles for women who were further from diagnosis. In addition, similar results were found for this group of women's distress from the symptoms of their cancer treatment.

Previous counseling. An interaction was found for the self-image subscale of the Problem Scale. The effect of receipt of the intervention on self-image was greater among women with previous counseling than among those without previous counseling.

DISCUSSION

Group Attendance

We found that implementing an intervention of this magnitude (25 groups) in a large geographical region creates logistical problems. Because of the size of the geographical area and the fact that the intervention focused on the first months following diagnosis, each woman had one chance to participate in the intervention. If she was not available when the group was scheduled or if she was unable or unwilling to go to the specific location of the sessions, then she could not participate. Initially, we did not take this into consideration in our randomization scheme. Of the 60 women who were randomized to the group intervention, but never came to groups, most were early participants. Most also reported high levels of self-esteem. Once this problem was recognized, the randomization procedure was changed to take the logistics of the scheduling into consideration.

We did find that once a woman came to the group, she generally stayed in the group. Only a small number of women (less than 15) who started the group came less than six times. Reasons for non-attendance were conflicts with work schedules, vacations, and treatment-related problems (either side effects of chemotherapy or, for a few women, a stem cell transplant).

Explanation of Findings

Consistent with our expectations, some women benefited more from the group than others. One group that benefited most were women who reported less emotional support at home. This finding is consistent with the work of other investigators (Helgeson et al., 1999; Antoni et al., 2001) who used different group interventions. In the study by Helgeson and her colleagues, the design compared education alone, support alone, or education and support with a no intervention control group. As reported earlier, the strongest intervention effect was in the didactic education group, the support and education group was next, followed by the support group alone. She also found interactions between women with low emotional support and the support group intervention. Some of her negative findings maybe explained by invidious comparisons made by women based on the number of positive lymph nodes. In our intervention, we prevented this from happening by indicating that all of the women were at risk for cancer recurrence. From a theoretical prospective, one can conclude that the expected positive benefit to women from making downward comparisons did not occur. Using a cognitive behavioral group intervention, Antoni and his colleagues (2001) found weak main effects from the intervention. They did find that the least optimistic women initially, became less depressed following the intervention.

One of theoretical notions behind a support group intervention is that having "similar others" to talk with provides support to women undergoing a difficult experience such as the diagnosis and treatment of breast cancer (Thoits, 1995). Taken together, these studies suggest that "similar others" is possibly equivalent to but not better than having emotionally supportive friends and relatives. For women who do not have these sources of support, the group fills the void.

A second aim of this study was to determine the optimal time for intervention. However, based on our Phase I data, we did not find that women experienced more problems immediately following diagnosis than they did at the end of treatment. Thus, we recruited women to participate who were within seven months of diagnosis. Our Phase Two results indicate that women who were further from diagnosis reported the greatest benefits from the group. This finding is consistent with our earlier study that during treatment, the woman feels cared for and supported by the medical and nursing staff. The cessation of active treatment makes the woman feel vulnerable to recurrence (Fobair et al., 1986). Once treatment has ended, support from the treatment staff (social workers, nurses, physicians) is reduced as well. Thus, group support the women receive from "similar others" replaces this loss of support (PABC, 1987).

Using a growth and development model, the psycho-educational intervention incorporates material from "behavior change" techniques. Educationally focused support groups are based on the premise that the more people know about their disease, treatment and side effects, the greater are their chances of achieving their maximum level of wellness. These groups are especially helpful for the newly diagnosed patients who are overwhelmed by technical information, barraged by having to learn a new medical language and by having to make critical medical decisions. Often this is the first formal "group" experience for the individual.

The results suggest the pitfalls in raising the consciousness of the women. The intervention may have helped women overcome denial and recognize their problems. By providing information to the women, their denial of the seriousness of their situation cannot be maintained (Bloom, et al., 1978). They are sensitized to issues such as interpersonal relationship problems and sexual problems. These data suggest that the intervention may not have been sufficiently long to develop the skills to resolve problems. Thus, the women who benefited most from the intervention were those who had previous counseling. That is, they already had the skills to help resolve the new problems that they were experiencing or they were troubled and needy (Antoni et al., 2001; Helgeson et al., 1999; 2001). These findings as well as the findings of the current study suggest that a longer intervention or one which meets at less frequent intervals, after an initial opportunity for the development of psychological bonding among participants and the introduction of problem solving skills, may be the answer. We did not find race/ethnic differences in the effects of the intervention between the women. This is less surprising given the findings of our focus groups suggesting that regardless of race/ethnicity, the women had a common bond based on their similarity of having a breast cancer diagnosis.

CONCLUSION

Of the women who participated in the psycho-educational support groups, the majority found the intervention "helpful" or "very helpful." However, when the results for participants were compared to women who did not receive the intervention, no main effects were found immediately following the end of the group sessions. Three months after the end of the intervention, group members reported more sexual problems and poorer mental health. The intervention, however, was effective for subgroups believed to be at greatest risk of psychological distress, women who perceived a lack of emotional support from family and friends. In addition, the intervention was effective for individuals who had received counseling in the past and those who were further from diagnosis.

ACKNOWLEDGEMENTS

We gratefully acknowledge the assistance of the interviewers for both phases of the study--Shelia Auzenne, Sally Balmer, Bobbi Braden, Rosalyn Britt, Alma Burrell, Eileen Chang, TiMoune Davis, Sherrie Elekwachi, Ann Keeler Evans, Gwen Moore, Natalia Rabin, Janice Smith-Yamagata, Rochelle Sullivan and Claire Silver. We also thank the following people who were facilitators of the psycho-educational support groups during the second phase of the study-- Mirna Alvarado, Sally Balmer, Barbara Ciserelli, Lien Cao, PhD, Ann Keeler Evans, Evan C. Wong-Kim LCSW, MPH, PhD, Angela Sun, MPH, Ollie Simpson, LCSW, Joyce Ting, LCSW and Marybeth Faustine. We are grateful to Susan Weisberg, LCSW who along with Pat Fobair, MPH, LCSW trained the group facilitators and was assisted by Wanna Wright, JD a cancer survivor. We thank Jeanne Quivey, MD, who provided radiation oncology input for the project, Monica Johnston, MS and Ingrid Peterson, MPH for their programming and statistical analysis, Carol Somkin, PhD for leading the analysis of the focus groups, and Merrilee Morrow for her development of the data base and project coordination. The National Cancer Institute, RO1 CA64730, supported this research.

REFERENCES

Antoni , M.H., Lehman, J.M., Kilbourn, K.M., Boyers, A.E., Culver, J.L., Alferi, S.M., Yount, S.E., McGregor, B.A., Arena, P.L., Harris, S.D., Price, A.A., Carver, C.S. Cognitive-behavioral stress management intervention decreases the prevalence of depression and enhances benefit finding among women under treatment for early-stage breast cancer. *Health Psychology*, 20(1): 20-32, 2001.

Block, G., Hartman, A.M., Naughton, D. A reduced dietary questionnaire: Development and validation. *Epidemiol* 1:58-64, 1990.

Bloom, J.R., Social support and adjustment to breast cancer. In: (Andersen BL, editor) *Women with Cancer: Psychological Perspectives*. Springer-Verlag, New York: pp. 204-209, 1986.

Bloom, J.B., D'Onofrio, C.A., Banks, P.J., Stewart, S.L., Johnston, m., Morrow, M., Fobair, P., Weisberg, S. A Psycho educational group intervention for young women with breast cancer: Design and process evaluation, Cancer *Research, Therapy and Control*, 8:93-102, 1999.

Bloom, J.R. and Kessler, L. The risk and timing of education and support interventions in young women with breast cancer. *J. Natl. Cancer Inst. Monograph*, 16:99-206, 1994.

Bloom, J.R., Ross, R.D. and Burnell, G.M., The effect of social support on patients adjustment following breast surgery, *Patient Counseling and Health Education*, 1(2) 50-59, 1978.

Bloom, J.R., Stewart, S.L., Banks, P.J., and Johnston, M., General and Specific Measures of Quality of Life in Young Women with Breast Cancer. In (Baum A and Andersen B, editors) Psychosocial Interventions for Cancer, American Psychological Association, Chapter 3, 37-56, 2000.

Bloom, J.R., Stewart, S.L., Johnston, M., Banks, P.J., Intrusiveness of illness and quality of life of young women with breast cancer. *Psycho-Oncology*, 7:(2) 89-100, 1998.

Bloom, J.R., Stewart, S.L., Johnston, M., Banks, P.J., and Fobair, P., Sources of support and the physical and mental well-being of young women with breast cancer, *Social Science and Medicine*, 53: 1513-1524 (2001).

Caplan, G., *Principles of Primary Prevention in Psychiatry*. Basic Books: New York, 1964.

Devins, G.M., Illness intrusiveness and the psychosocial impact of lifestyle disruption in chronic life-threatening disease. *Advances in Renal Replacement Therapy*, 1(3) 251- 264, 1994.

Edmonds, C.V.I, Lockwood, G.A., Cunningham, A.J. Psychological response to long-term therapy: a randomized trail with metastatic breast cancer patients. *Psycho-Oncology*, 8:73-91, 1999.

Ell, K., Nishimoto, R., Morvay, T., Mantell, J, Hamovitch, M. A longitudinal analysis of psychological adaptation among survivors of cancer, *Cancer*, 11:101-130, 1989.

Flamer, D.F., *Emotional Support Scale*, West Coast Cancer Foundation, 1975.

Flaskerud, J.H. Matching client and therapist ethnicity, language, and gender: A review of research. *Issues in Mental Health Nursing*, 11(4) 321-336, 1990.

Fobair, P., Hoppe, H., Bloom, J.R., Cox, R., Varghese, A., Spiegel, D., Psychosocial problems among survivors of Hodgkin's disease. *Journal of Clinical Oncology, 4(5)* 805-814, 1986.

Gaskin, T.A., LoBuglio, A., Kelly, P., Doss, M., Pizitz, N., STRETCH: rehabilitation program for patients with breast cancer. *Southeren Medical Journal*, 82:467-469, 1989.

Ganz, P.A., Patient education as a moderator of psychological distress. *Journal of Psychosocial Oncology.* 6:181-197, 1988.

Ganz, P.A., Coscarelli, A., Fred, C., Kahn. B., Polinsky, M.L. and Petersen, L. Breast cancer survivors: Psychosocial concerns and quality of life. *Breast Cancer Research and Treatment* 38: 183-199, 1996.

Ganz, P.A., Desmond, K.A., Leedham, B., Rowland, J.H., Meyerowitz, B.E., Belin T.R., Quality of life in long-term disease-free survivors of breast cancer: a follow-up study. *J. Natl. Cancer Inst.* 94:39-49, 2002.

Goodwin, P.J. et al. The effect of group psychosocial support on survival in metastatic breast cancer. *New England Journal of Medicine*, 345: 1719-1726, 2001.

Gottlieb, B.H.and Wachala, E.D. Cancer Support groups: A critical review of empirical studies. *Psycho-Oncology*: 16(5) 379-400, 2007.

Greater Bay Area Cancer Registry Report 1996: 6,1.

Helgeson,V.S., Cohen, S., Shultz, R., Yasko, J. Education and peer discussion group interventions and adjustment to breast cancer. *Archives of General Psychiatry*, 56:340- 347, 1999.

Helgeson, V.S, Cohen, S., Shultz, R., Yasko, J. Long-term effects of educational and peer discussion groups on adjustment to women with breast cancer, *Health Psychology*, 20: 387-292, 2001.

Jacobs, C., Ross, R.D, Walker, I.M., Stockdale, F.E., Behavior of cancer patients: A randomized study of education and peer support groups. *American Journal of Clinical Oncology*, 6:347- 350, 1983.

Kissane, D.W., Grabsch, B., Clarke, D.M. et al. Supportive-expressive group therapy: the transformation of existential ambivalence into creative living while enhancing adherence to anti-cancer therapies. *Psycho-Oncology*, 12: 755-768.

Kohout, F.J., Berkman, L.F., Evans, D.A., Coroni-Huntley, J., Two shorter forms of the CES-D-Depression Symptoms Index. *Journal of Aging and Health* 5(2) 179-193, 1993.

Lapore, S.J., Helgeson, V., Eton, D.T., Schultz, R., Improving quality of life in men with prostate cancer: A randomized controlled trial of group education interventions. *Health Psychology*, 2:443-452, 2003.

Lewis, F.M., Attributions of control, experienced learning and psychosocial well being Patients with advanced cancer *Journal of Psychosocial Oncology* 7:105-119, 1989.

Osteen, R.T., Cady, B., Friedman, M., Kraybill, W., Doggett, S., Hussey, D., Urist, M., Chmiel, J., Winchester, C.R., Patterns of care for younger women with breast cancer. *J. Natl. Cancer Inst. Monograph* 16:43-46, 1994.

PABC: Bloom, J.R., Cook, M., Fotopoulis, S., Flamer D, Gates C, Holland JC, Muenz, L., Murawski, .B, Penman, D., and Ross, R.D., Psychological response to mastectomy. *Cancer*, 59: 189-196, 1987.

Qaseem. A., Snow, V., Sherif, K., Aronson, M., Weiss. K.B., Owens, D.K., Screening mammography for women 40 to 49 years of age: a clinical practice guideline from the American College of Physicians. *Ann. Intern. Med.* 146:511-515, 2007.

Quivey, J., Luce, J.M., Stewart, S.L., Johnston, M., Banks, P.J., Bloom, J.R., Younger women with breast cancer: Patterns of care in 5 San Francisco Bay Area Counties. *Proceedings American Society of Clinical Oncology 17, Abstract 643, p. 167a, 1998.*

Radloff. L.S. The CES-D scale; A self-report depression scale for research in the general population. *Applied Psychological Measurement* 1:385-401, 1977.

Ries, L.A.G., Melbert, D., Krapcho, M., Mariotto, A., Miller, B.A., Feuer, E.J., Clegg, L., Horner, M.J., Howlader, N., Eisner, M.P., Reichman, M., Edwards, B.K. (eds). SEER Cancer Statistics Review, 1975-2004, National Cancer Institute. Bethesda, MD, http://seer. cancer.gov/csr/1975_2004/, based on November 2006 SEER data submission, posted to the SEER web site, 2007.

Rosenberg, M., Society *and adolescent self image*. Princeton, N J, Princeton University Press, 1965.

Satariano, W.A., Rageb, N.E., Branch, L.G., Swanson, G.M., Difficulties in physical function reported by middle aged and elderly women with breast cancer: A case control comparison. *Journal of Gerontology*, 45(1) M3-Mll, 1990.

Schain, W., *Breast Cancer Problems Checklist*, unpublished, 1979.

Shapiro, C.L., Recht, A. Late effects of adjuvant therapy for breast cancer. *J. Natl. Cancer Inst Monograph* 16:101-112, 1994.

Simpson, J., Carlson, L., Beck, C., Patten, S., Effects of a brief intervention on social support and psychiatric morbidity in breast cancer patients. *Psycho-Oncology*, 11:282-294, 2002.

Somkin, C.P., Otero-Sabogal, .R, Lampkin, S.M., McBride, M., Lee, M., Johnston, M., Stewart, S.L. Using focus groups to develop an intervention for multiethnic younger women with breast cancer, unpublished manuscript.

Spiegel, D.S. and Bloom, J.R., Group Therapy and Hypnosis Reduce Breast Cancer Pain: A Randomized Prospective Outcome Study. *Psychosomatic Medicine, 45*:333-339, 1983.

Spiegel, D.S., Bloom, J.R., Yalom, I, Group support for patients with metastatic breast cancer: A randomized prospective outcome study. *Archives of General Psychiatry*, 38:527-533, 1981.

Spiegel, D.S., Bloom, J.R., Kraemer, H.C., Gottheil, E., Effect of psychosocial treatment on survival of patients with metastatic breast cancer. *Lancet*, 2; 888-891, 1989.

Telch, C.F., Telch, M.J., Group coping skills instruction and supportive group therapy for cancer patients: A comparison of strategies. *Journal of Consulting and Clinical Psychology,* 54: 802-808, 1986.

Thoits, P., Stress, coping and social support processes: Where are we? What next? *Journal of Health and Social Behavior.* Extra Issue; 53-79.1995.

Trijsburg, R.W., van Knippenberg, F.C.E., and Rijpma, S.E. Effects of psychological treatment on cancer patients: A critical review. *Psychosomatic Medicine,* re, 489-517, 1992.

Ware, J.E. Jr., Sherbourne, C.D., The MOS 36 item short-form survey (SF-36). *Med Care,* 30:473-483, 1992.

In: Psychological Counseling Research Focus
Editors: James A. Patterson et al, pp. 47-58

ISBN 978-1-60456-041-1
© 2008 Nova Science Publishers, Inc.

Chapter 3

A MODEL OF EDUCATIONAL VIDEO INTERVENTION FOR PREVENTIVE CARE IN THE EMERGENCY DEPARTMENT

Yvette Calderon, Ethan Cowan and Marianne Haughey
Department of Emergency Medicine, Jacobi Medical Center,
Albert Einstein College of Medicine, Bronx, NY, USA

ABSTRACT

The role of emergency departments (EDs) in providing patients with preventive services remains controversial; however, it is clear that vulnerable communities including minority, elderly and low income patients, seek out the ED for their primary medical care. For these vulnerable patient populations, the emergency department serves as a "safety net", providing essential health care needs to those most at risk patients, who may have limited or no access to regular medical services. For these at risk patients the emergency department can provide essential education on preventive health measures. Studies have demonstrated that, as part of their emergency care, patients both need and desire information on preventive health issues.[1] While the arguments to provide health information and preventive services are persuasive there are legitimate barriers to providing these services in the emergency department such as time, responsibility and resources. The use of video as a tool for health education may help to diminish the barriers to effective health education for emergency department patients. Video offers several benefits over oral conveyance of information including: the consistency of information delivery, the ability to provide the tool in different languages, and the ability to utilize this method while the patient waits in the emergency department. Video effectiveness can also be enhanced as an educational tool by developing video interventions using a theoretical framework and a multidisciplinary approach. This approach can be used for any preventive care service that an emergency department patient population would need. This chapter will demonstrate how theory based educational videos can, and have been used successfully to educate emergency department patients, especially those with limited literacy or limited proficiency with the English language.

BACKGROUND

Emergency Departments (EDs) commonly care large numbers of medically underserved patients.[2] These "priority populations" often do not seek care in other health care environments due to socioeconomics, lack of insurance or immigration status. Often, these patient populations are disproportionately poor minorities and non-English speaking. While these "priority populations" utilize health care at a lower frequency, they are at higher risk for many common diseases that carry high rates of morbidity and mortality. Often, complications of these inadequately managed medical conditions lead them to seek care in the emergency department setting. Once in the emergency department, providers have a unique opportunity to educate patients about preventive care, and link them to an appropriate health care setting. Unfortunately, in busy emergency department setting providers rarely have the time to properly educate patients. The medical needs of other patients compete for providers' valuable time, and the growing problem of emergency department overcrowding limits this time even further.[3, 4] Video is one potential way to reduce the provider time required to convey complex preventive health messages and ensure the delivery of clear and concise preventive health information and education efficiently to all patients. The use of video and education has already proven successful in different medical settings; however, the successful use of media and its development must involve theory and linguistic and cultural competency as well as potential limits in patient's health literacy. Our institution has developed a model using educational theory based videos that successfully conveys preventive health information to emergency department patients.

Definition of Health Education

Health education involves the communication of information and the teaching of skills needed to improve ones individual health and well being. Health education is defined by the World Health Organization as education that, "comprises consciously constructed opportunities for learning involving some form of communication designed to improve *health literacy*, including improving knowledge, and developing *life skills* which are conducive to individual and *community health*."[5]

Tailoring of Health Education to Specific Patient Populations

Ideally, health education would be directed at people who would be most expected to benefit from an educational intervention. When health education programs have been tailored to specific populations significant improvement in understanding of health information have been achieved.[6-18] One model target population are patients who have limited contact with the health care system who are frequently excluded from health education interventions. Often times, these patients only contact with the healthcare system is in the emergency department, thus, this setting provides a irreplaceable opportunity to use educational interventions for improving patient's health and well-being. Even in the emergency department, the educational message can be missed if the educator does not take into consideration the target population's level of health literacy, their primary language, and how much time they might realistically be able to devote to educational sessions.

Developing Educational Theory Based Videos

In developing patient education videos it is essential to take educational theory into account in order to make the intervention as effective as possible. While there are many educational theories that can be used when developing educational intervention tools, the videos used in our department were based on two educational theories; constructivism and the theory of meaningful learning.

One method of learning is to use one's interactions with the environment and experiences to "construct" one's knowledge. This is the basis of the theory of Constructivism. There are three important cognitive processes during knowledge construction which can explained with the SOI model: S for selecting relevant information, O for organizing incoming information and I for integrating incoming information. Knowledge is constructed by the learner as they process their experiences.[19] Learners make sense of the presented materials to make their own relevant knowledge.[20, 21] They also need to identify and pursue their learning goals. A constructivist focuses on "learning in context".[19] For this to be effective, the context must be meaningful to the individual.

New concepts are incorporated into the knowledge that individuals already have. The "Theory of Meaningful Learning" is defined as the process of relating meaningful information to what the learner already knows in a precise and significant way.[22] There are three conditions that need to be met in meaningful learning: 1) the learner must employ a meaningful learning set, 2) the information must be meaningful and relevant and 3) the information must relate to what the learner already knows.[22]

Prior knowledge plays an important role in the meaningful learning theory. There is a very important distinction between receptive learning and discovery when discussing meaningful learning. Receptive learning is usually presented in a formal didactic learning style, while discovery learning the learner plays an active role in internalizing the material. Therefore the learning material must be explicitly organized, and relevant to the learner.[22]

General Use of Video in Health Education

The use of video has become more prevalent in the education of patients, and has become an alternative method to providing screening and prevention services to high-risk patient populations.[9, 23, 24] Video, as a teaching tool, has been shown to be effective at many levels in the health care system. Videotaped presentations are effective in the education of patients regarding diverse topics, such as smoking cessation, elective cardiac surgery and consenting for HIV testing.[23-25] Video also results in better knowledge retention [9, 26, 27],28and has been shown to increase patient satisfaction with their healthcare visit [29]. Studies regarding video education specific to HIV have shown that the use of video containing information about HIV risk reduction is a cost effective way to reduce risk among males with multiple partners.[30] Studies on providing patients with information about colonoscopy have also demonstrated that, when given the choice between oral, written, or video presentation of health information, patients preferred the video format over the other options. Patients found that a video presentation made the information easier to understand and provided the appropriate amount of information.[25, 31]

Health Education in the Emergency Department Population

Despite the success of health education programs in other health care settings there continues to be debate about their use in the Emergency Department.[32] One reason for this debate is that the Emergency Department setting and patient population present significant challenges to the development and implementation of successful health education programs. These challenges involve a nonconductive physical plant, emergency department overcrowding, competing patient care responsibilities, and a challenging patient population.

The physical plants of many emergency departments' are not conducive to educational sessions. The Emergency Department is frequently loud and chaotic. Additional, the census can be highly variable, and depending on the amount of overcrowding, patient privacy can be severely limited. Emergency department overcrowding, by itself, can also hinder effective implementation of health education programs. For example, in an overcrowded emergency department patient-physician communication, a central component to health education, is limited. This limitation of "face-to-face" time between the patients and their health care providers leaves little time for effective health education. One obvious problem is that in an overcrowded emergency department there simply is not enough time for the provider to convey the complex health education information to patients. [3, 4]

Competing patient care responsibilities present another challenge to implementing health education programs. Emergency department physicians already have multiple competing responsibilities as they care for patients. The physician is required to conduct patient interviews, physical exams, process laboratory and radiographic data for multiple patients simultaneously. In addition to theses clinical duties the physician frequently is responsible for the flow of patients through the emergency department, proper medical documentation, and other administrative tasks. In academic centers, emergency physicians have the added responsibility of supervising residents. This level of multitasking leaves little time for effective implementation of health education interventions that require a time commitment from the physician. Complex information takes precious time to deliver, and in the throes of an ED busy with patients whose health issues are more immediate, prevention messages often take a back seat to current issues. [3, 4]

Lastly, emergency department patients themselves present a unique challenge to the implementation of effective health education programs. Studies have shown that emergency department patients may have low health literacy levels that hinder their ability to understand preventive health information.[39-42] Despite lower health literacy levels these patients are often required to absorb large volumes of technical medical information regarding their disease conditions during a brief emergency department visit. Often, patients with the greatest health burdens are not able to fully interpret and understand the complex health terminology and instructions. In emergency department patients with poor health literacy, provider initiated health education may be compromised by the patient's inability to understand this information.

Non-English speaking patients offer an additional challenge, requiring more provider time and greater use of ancillary resources. Over 46 million people in the United States claim a non-English language as their primary language, and more than 21 million speak English less than "very well."[33] Most health care organizations provide either inadequate interpreter services or no services at all.[34-38] The lack of adequate translation services limits a provider's ability to provide health education.

In spite of the challenges the emergency department presents a unique opportunity to educate patients. Frequently, the emergency department may be a patient's only point of contact with the health care system because uninsured patients regularly use the emergency department as their source of primary care.[32, 43, 44] These patients may have acute exacerbations of chronic diseases such as asthma, diabetes, and coronary artery disease that bring them into contact with the emergency department physician. In an acute phase of disease activity these patients may be more receptive to health education, a phenomenon referred to as the "teachable moment".[45] In designing a system to provide important and complex information to these often receptive patients, video has significant advantages.

Implementing Video Education in the Emergency Department

A variety educational videos can be produced for use in the emergency department setting. These videos can be used for a wide array of purposes such as providing disease specific information, assisting with decision making regarding treatment options, improving coping skills and teaching self care practices. In our emergency department the goal was to produce videos to provide pre-test information for HIV testing and to assist in the informed consent process for a common emergency department procedure, intravenous contrast administration for computed tomography.

The educational HIV pretest counseling videos developed by Calderon, et. al.[25] for an inner city patient population were designed to give essential HIV testing information that a patient would need prior to making an informed decision on HIV testing. The videos were developed using the theories of constructivism and meaningful learning previously described and were organized so that patients could visualize scenarios of patient encounters and how meaningful and relevant HIV testing information was processed. The HIV testing video contained all the essential elements of a pre-test counseling session: HIV transmission, nature and meaning of the HIV test, benefits to testing, reporting, partner notification and the definition of voluntary and mandatory testing. The video was available in English and Spanish and dubbed in French and Albanian. After development, the video was tested in a prospective randomized control trial comparing the educational effectiveness of the video to the usual practice of an informational session with an HIV counselor. The study demonstrated that the HIV educational/ informed consent video was at least as effective as a in-person pretest counselor in conveying information related to HIV testing.[25]

A second randomized control trial used the HIV testing video to provide pre-test counseling information between the hours of 4pm-12pm weekdays and on weekends when HIV counselors were unavailable. If no video was available, the standard of care was to refer the patient to an HIV counselor during the next available normal business hours. The study demonstrated that when the video was used, patients who presented during evenings and weekends, when there were no HIV counselors available, were more likely to get tested.

Patients who told to return for in-person counseling with an HIV counselor during normal business were less likely to get tested. [46]

The second use of video in our emergency department was to assist in the informed consent process for a common emergency department procedure, intravenous contrast (IV) administration for computed tomography. Obtaining informed consent is a complex issue, made more difficult by the challenges of the emergency department. Providing the necessary information to obtained adequate Informed consent is a time consuming procedure. Providers in the emergency department are often rushed and their attention may be diverted away from providing the necessary informed consent information by other patient care needs. Patients, on the other hand, are worried about their acute issue and may hesitate to ask questions. Providing complex medical information to non-English speaking emergency department patients and those with limited functional literacy during the informed consent process offers additional challenges.

Video assisted informed consent may be a practical solution to enhance patients' understanding of medical information used in the informed consent process and offers one practical alternative to physician provided information. Video has the advantage of providing clear and concise information, in a reproducible manner, efficiently to all patients regardless of primary language. Developed appropriately, educational videos used in the informed consent process can improve patients' understanding of medical information. Patients with limited literacy and English fluency may benefit to a greater extent in regards to knowledge acquisition than English speakers.

We developed a video to assist in the informed consent process of IV contrast administration for computed tomography. The IV contrast video contained information in English or Spanish on the risks, benefits and alternatives to receiving IV contrast for computed tomography. This video was used in a randomized controlled trial to determine if these educational videos were superior to routine discussion for informing patients about risks, benefits, and alternatives to receiving IV contrast for computed tomography. In this study patients either watched a video in Spanish or English explaining the procedure and its risks, benefits, and alternatives or underwent routine discussion, receiving IV contrast information from their physician. After their educational sessions, all participants completed a knowledge measure.

Patient in the video assisted informed consent group achieved higher mean knowledge scores compared to patients receiving routine discussion. Both English and Spanish speaking patients who received video assisted informed consent scored higher than English and Spanish speakers who discussed IV contrast administration with their physician. Spanish speaking patients who watched the video in their language achieved a level of understanding comparable to their English-speaking counterparts. Patient in the video group also exhibited greater satisfaction than patients in the routine discussion group. No patients refused administration of IV contrast.

The HIV video and IV contrast video studies had proven benefit for patients in our emergency department. Patients who watched either video consistently scored better that those provided information by practitioners. The videos were available in the two primary languages spoken in our emergency department patient population, English and Spanish. The availability of bilingual videos enabled Spanish speakers to receive the same information as their English speaking counterparts without the need, cost and hassle of additional translation services. Patients in our emergency department were satisfied with the use of video in both the HIV testing and informed consent scenarios. Thus, in these two aforementioned studies it appeared that the use of video education resulted in improved understanding of health information for our emergency department patients.

Advantages of Video Education in the Emergency Department Setting

Video Instruction as a Time Saver in the Emergency Department

Educational videos have the advantage of being able to consistently deliver clear and concise information efficiently and to all patients. The use of educational videos shifts the role of the emergency department provider from the source of primary information to the expert answering questions arising from the video. The time savings gained from the videos allow the emergency department physician to spend more time on primary patient care responsibilities. This time savings is also the primary reason for the proven cost effectiveness of video education.[30] The video can also be administered such a way that it does not delay patient's care. In 2003, emergency department patients waited an average of 46 minutes to see a physician and typically spend 3 or more hours in the department undergoing medical evaluation and stabilization.[30] These waits can be even longer in the inner-city urban emergency departments. If admitted to the hospital, these patients may wait much longer in the emergency department until an inpatient bed becomes available. The time that a patient spends in the emergency department provides ample opportunity for patients to view educational videos.

Video Instruction for non-English Speaking Emergency Department Patients

Multilingual educational videos are one potential alternative to providing preventive health information to non-English speaking patients. Prior studies demonstrate that multilingual videos can improve non-English speaking patients' understanding of medical information.[47] Multilingual videos can also reduce the need for costly and time consuming telephone translation services or inappropriate use of unqualified staff or family members. The videos are also available during non-business hours thus reducing the problem of finding qualified translators when institutional translators are absent. Improved communication as a result of multilingual preventive healthcare videos may even help to reduce dangerous health behaviors in non-English speaking patient population.

Video Instruction for Emergency Department Patients with Limited Literacy

Adult literacy continues to be a major problem in the Unites States. In 1993, the National Adult Literacy Survey reported that 40 to 44 million Americans, or approximately one quarter of the US population, were functionally illiterate.[48] Another 50 million had marginal literacy skills, meaning that almost half of the adult US population had limited or low literacy skills. Minority, non-English speakers, the elderly and the poor face literacy problems more commonly.[49, 50] Prior studies of emergency department patients also demonstrate that this patient population has limited functional literacy.[40, 41] Educational videos can be created using standardized vocabulary and sentence structure that is comprehensible at a low literacy level. The strength of the video presentation for patients with low literacy levels lies in its consistency and delivery. Unlike emergency department providers who exhibit variability in their ability to deliver health information at an understandable level, the video provides the same information at the same level of comprehension for all patients. Furthermore, the video can be developed such that patients are able to repeat sections or informational "chapters" that they do not understand. Formal testing of comprehension can also be incorporated into the videos to test patients understanding. Patients who score poorly on formal testing can then be prompted to review the material prior to proceeding on to subsequent informational "chapters". Using standardized video scripts geared toward patients with low literacy levels and incorporating formal knowledge testing, educational videos can provide useful information to all patients regardless of their literacy level.

Disadvantages of Video Education In the Emergency Department Setting

Production of educational videos can be expensive. Professional productions can cost upwards of $10,000 per minute of video. Previously commercially developed educational videos are available from multiple companies; however, these videos can be expensive and are often not geared toward non-English speaking patients or those with low literacy levels. They may also not address the specific topics relevant to the particular population you wish to educate. Non-professional video production can reduce costs; however, multiple considerations must be taken into account when producing your own educational videos.[51] For example, decisions must be made about filming location; use of professional actors versus actual physicians or patients; scripted scenes versus improvisation; single versus multiple cameras; and professional editing versus commonly available computer editing software. Each level of increased sophistication in video production results in increased cost.

Significant cost reduction in video production can be achieved by using hospital based resources. For example, the videos used in our Emergency Department were produced by the audio-visual staff of our hospital using a hand-held digital video recorder. With digital video recording the video can be uploaded into a multimedia computer workstation where a skilled technician can edit the video using commonly available software. Incorporation of knowledge based assessments requires the additional expertise of a computer programmer with experience in multimedia design. While less sophisticated videos can be shown on portable DVD players at a patient's bedside, more complex multimedia videos must be shown on template or laptop computers increasing overall costs.

The second disadvantage of video education in the emergency department is the absence of "human" adaptability in the education process. Videos cannot anticipate or adjust to individuals learning needs; instead they present information the same way to all patients. Therefore the consistency that is one of the advantages of video can also be a disadvantage. One method to reduce this potential shortcoming is to re-introduce the provider to answer questions that the videos produce. The providers' role shifts from the supplier of primary information to the expert answering questions that arise from the video.

SUMMARY AND CONCLUSION

Health education in the emergency department is complicated by multiple factors. Competing patient care responsibilities, lack of adequate time for educational activities, and a patient population with poor health literacy and English proficiency make developing and implementing effective educational interventions incredibly challenging. Despite these challenges, emergency department patients may be most in need of preventive health education.

Educational videos can be developed and used to overcome many of the challenges to patient education present in the emergency department setting. Our experience with video education for two carefully selected educational topics has been impressive. Our department is providing HIV testing in a manner considerate to the time constraints of the emergency department practitioner while providing a useful and essential community service. The use of the IV consent video has allowed us to provide consistent information to patients about a complex topic in a language in which they are comfortable. The IV contrast video ensures that all patients are provided with enough information about the procedure so that they can make a truly informed decision.

The use of educational videos in the emergency department is still in its infancy. There are a wide range of topics that might be well suited to the development of video and applicability to the emergency department patient population. There are some obstacles in developing educational video programs but, we have found that the benefits of video education outweigh the difficulties. The value of providing consistent information, in languages that are accessible to our patients in way that is also considerate of varying patient literacy can not be overestimated. Patients clearly welcomed the video interventions into their care, and practitioners are satisfied by the time-savings these videos provide. Our studies lend validity to the future development of this genre of video education.

REFERENCES

[1] Rodriguez Rm Fau - Kreider WJ, Kreider Wj Fau - Baraff LJ, Baraff LJ. Need and desire for preventive care measures in emergency department patients. (0196-0644 (Print)).

[2] McCaig LF, Burt CW. National Hospital Ambulatory Medical Care Survey: 2002 emergency department summary. *Adv. Data.* Mar 18 2004(340):1-34.

[3] Derlet R, Richards J, Kravitz R. Frequent overcrowding in U.S. emergency departments. *Acad. Emerg. Med.* Feb 2001;8(2):151-155.

[4] Thompson DA, Yarnold PR, Williams DR, et al. Effects of actual waiting time, perceived waiting time, information delivery, and expressive quality on patient satisfaction in the emergency department. *Ann. Emerg. Med.* Dec 1996;28(6):657-665.

[5] Smith BJ, Tang KC, Nutbeam D. WHO Health Promotion Glossary: new terms. *Health Promot. Int.* Dec 2006;21(4):340-345.

[6] Cull A, Miller H, Porterfield T, et al. The use of videotaped information in cancer genetic counselling: a randomized evaluation study. *Br. J. Cancer.* Mar. 1998;77(5):830-837.

[7] Dunn RA, Shenouda PE, Martin DR, et al. Videotape increases parent knowledge about poliovirus vaccines and choices of polio vaccination schedules. *Pediatrics.* Aug. 1998;102(2):e26.

[8] Schapira MM, Meade C, Nattinger AB. Enhanced decision-making: the use of a videotape decision-aid for patients with prostate cancer. *Patient Educ. Couns.* Feb. 1997;30(2):119-127.

[9] Weston J, Hannah M, Downes J. Evaluating the benefits of a patient information video during the informed consent process. *Patient Educ. Couns.* Mar. 1997;30(3):239-245.

[10] Lin PC, Lin LC, Lin JJ. Comparing the effectiveness of different educational programs for patients with total knee arthroplasty. *Orthop. Nurs.* Sep.-Oct. 1997;16(5):43-49.

[11] Lisko SA. Development and use of videotaped instruction for preoperative education of the ambulatory gynecological patient. *J. Post Anesth. Nurs.* Dec. 1995;10(6):324-328.

[12] McDaniel RW, Rhodes VA. Development of a preparatory sensory information videotape for women receiving chemotherapy for breast cancer. *Cancer Nurs.* Apr. 1998;21(2):143-148.

[13] Meade CD, McKinney WP, Barnas GP. Educating patients with limited literacy skills: the effectiveness of printed and videotaped materials about colon cancer. *Am. J. Public Health.* Jan. 1994;84(1):119-121.

[14] Mynaugh PA. A randomized study of two methods of teaching perineal massage: effects on practice rates, episiotomy rates, and lacerations. *Birth.* Sep. 1991;18(3):153-159.

[15] O'Donnell L, San Doval A, Duran R, et al. The effectiveness of video-based interventions in promoting condom acquisition among STD clinic patients. *Sex Transm. Dis.* Mar.-Apr. 1995;22(2):97-103.

[16] Robinson P, Katon W, Von Korff M, et al. The education of depressed primary care patients: what do patients think of interactive booklets and a video? *J. Fam. Pract.* Jun. 1997;44(6):562-571.

[17] Steinberg TG, Diercks MJ, Millspaugh J. An evaluation of the effectiveness of a videotape for discharge teaching of organ transplant recipients. *J Transpl Coord.* Jun 1996;6(2):59-63.

[18] Wood RY. Breast self-examination proficiency in older women: measuring the efficacy of video self-instruction kits. *Cancer Nurs.* Dec. 1996;19(6):429-436.

[19] Driscoll M. *Psychology of Learning for Instruction.* 3rd ed. Boston, MA: Allyn and Bacon; 2005.

[20] Smith P, Ragan T. *Instructional Design.* 2nd ed. New York, New York: Wiley; 1999.

[21] Mayer R. Designing instruction for constructivist learning. *Instructional design theories and models: A new paradigm of instructional theory.* Vol 2. Mahwah, NJ: Lawrence Erlbaum; 1999:141-159.

[22] Driscoll M. *Psychology of learning for instruction.* 3rd ed. Boston, MA: Allyn and Bacon; 2005.

[23] May S, West R, Hajek P, et al. The use of videos to inform smokers about different nicotine replacement products. *Patient Educ. Couns.* Oct. 2003;51(2):143-147.

[24] Roth-Isigkeit A, Ocklitz E, Bruckner S, et al. Development and evaluation of a video program for presentation prior to elective cardiac surgery. *Acta Anaesthesiol. Scand.* Apr. 2002;46(4):415-423.

[25] Calderon Y, Haughey M, Bijur PE, et al. An educational HIV pretest counseling video program for off-hours testing in the emergency department. *Ann. Emerg. Med.* Jul. 2006;48(1):21-27.

[26] Reznik M, Sharif I, Ozuah PO. Use of interactive videoconferencing to deliver asthma education to inner-city immigrants. *J. Telemed. Telecare.* 2004;10(2):118-120.

[27] Cowan EA, Calderon Y, Gennis P, et al. Spanish and English video-assisted informed consent for intravenous contrast administration in the emergency department: a randomized controlled trial. *Ann. Emerg. Med.* Feb. 2007;49(2):221-230, 230 e221-223.

[28] Fureman I, Meyers K, McLellan AT, et al. Evaluation of a video-supplement to informed consent: injection drug users and preventive HIV vaccine efficacy trials. *AIDS Educ. Prev.* Aug .1997;9(4):330-341.

[29] Oermann MH. Effects of educational intervention in waiting room on patient satisfaction. *J. Ambul. Care Manage.* Apr.-Jun. 2003;26(2):150-158.

[30] Sweat M, O'Donnell C, O'Donnell L. Cost-effectiveness of a brief video-based HIV intervention for African American and Latino sexually transmitted disease clinic clients. *AIDS.* Apr. 13 2001;15(6):781-787.

[31] Agre P, Kurtz RC, Krauss BJ. A randomized trial using videotape to present consent information for colonoscopy. *Gastrointest. Endosc.* May-June 1994;40(3):271-276.

[32] Rhodes KV, Gordon JA, Lowe RA. Preventive care in the emergency department, Part I: Clinical preventive services--are they relevant to emergency medicine? Society for Academic Emergency Medicine Public Health and Education Task Force Preventive Services Work Group. *Acad. Emerg. Med.* Sep. 2000;7(9):1036-1041.

[33] Profile of Selected Social Characteristics. In: Bureau UC, ed. 2000.

[34] ASTHO Bilingual Health Initiative: Report and Recommendations. In: Health OoM, ed. 1992.

[35] Need for interpreter/translation services critical in hospitals and other clinical settings. *Health Care Strateg. Manage.* Jun. 1995;13(6):15.

[36] Baker DW, Parker RM, Williams MV, et al. Use and effectiveness of interpreters in an emergency department. *JAMA.* Mar. 13 1996;275(10):783-788.

[37] Ginsberg C, Martin D, Andrulis D, et al. Interpretation and Translation Services in Health Care: A Survey of US Public and Private Teaching Hospitals. 1995.

[38] Schmidt R, Ahart A, Shur G. *Limited English Proficiency as a Barrier to Health and Social Services.* Washington D. C.: Macro Interaction, Inc.; 1995.

[39] Powers RD. Emergency department patient literacy and the readability of patient-directed materials. *Ann. Emerg. Med.* Feb. 1988;17(2):124-126.

[40] Jolly BT, Scott JL, Feied CF, et al. Functional illiteracy among emergency department patients: a preliminary study. *Ann. Emerg. Med.* Mar. 1993;22(3):573-578.

[41] Spandorfer JM, Karras DJ, Hughes LA, et al. Comprehension of discharge instructions by patients in an urban emergency department. *Ann. Emerg. Med.* Jan. 1995;25(1):71-74.

[42] Williams DM, Counselman FL, Caggiano CD. Emergency department discharge instructions and patient literacy: a problem of disparity. *Am. J. Emerg. Med.* Jan. 1996;14(1):19-22.

[43] Bernstein E, Goldfrank LR, Kellerman AL, et al. A public health approach to emergency medicine: preparing for the twenty-first century. *Acad. Emerg. Med.* May-June 1994;1(3):277-286.

[44] Bernstein E, Bernstein J. *Case Studies in Emergency Medicine and Health of the Public*. Boston: Jones and Bartlett; 1996.

[45] Bowling JR. Clinical teaching in the ambulatory care setting: how to capture the teachable moment. *J. Am. Osteopath. Assoc.* Feb .1993;93(2):235-239.

[46] Calderon Y. Increasing Willingness to be Tested for HIV in the Emergency Department During Off Hour Tours: A Randomized Trial. *Academic Emergency Medicine*. 2005;Abstract.

[47] Borrayo EA. Where's Maria? A video to increase awareness about breast cancer and mammography screening among low-literacy Latinas. *Prev. Med.* July 2004;39(1):99-110.

[48] Irwin S, Kirsch A. Adult Literacy in America: A First Look at the Findings of the National Adult Literacy Survey. 1993.

[49] Campbell FA, Goldman BD, Boccia ML, et al. The effect of format modifications and reading comprehension on recall of informed consent information by low-income parents: a comparison of print, video, and computer-based presentations. *Patient Educ. Couns.* May 2004;53(2):205-216.

[50] Williams MV, Parker RM, Baker DW, et al. Inadequate functional health literacy among patients at two public hospitals. *JAMA*. Dec. 6 1995;274(21):1677-1682.

[51] Pinsky LE, Wipf JE. A picture is worth a thousand words: practical use of videotape in teaching. *J. Gen. Intern. Med.* Nov. 2000;15(11):805-810.

Chapter 4

GRADUATE COUNSELING STUDENTS SUCCESS COUNSELING UNDERGRADUATE STUDENTS AS CLIENTS: A MODEL FOR TRAINING

Maureen C. Kenny
Florida International University, College of Education,
Department of Educational and Psychological Studies,
Miami, Florida, USA

ABSTRACT

Ensuring that counselors-in-training learn the clinical skills necessary to be effective counselors prior to field placements is a major concern for faculty. This paper highlights how undergraduate volunteer clients can be utilized in the training of graduate students enrolled in an advanced counseling skills course. Results of this study demonstrate how effective this training modality was, with clients reporting a positive experience with the counseling sessions. Additionally, the counselors-in-training described the experience as realistic and more beneficial than role playing with a classmate. This data also demonstrates that clients can be helped with their difficulties in a rather short period of time by counselors-in-training. Recommendations for using this method, as well as limitations, are addressed.

Ensuring that counselors-in-training learn counseling skills necessary to be effective is a goal of every counseling training program. Despite the agreement among educators that it is essential to teach such skills, there is little written about how to proceed with this task and ensure that counselors-in-training are appropriately prepared. Many experiential methods have been used in the training process including watching videos, modeling by faculty, practicing with peers, in class simulation experiences (e.g., role plays), supervised practice, use of actors to portray clients, and teaching micro skills (Ivey and Bradford Ivey, 2007; Levitov, Fall and Jennings, 1999; Osborn, Daninhirsch and Page, 2003; Osborn, Dean and Petruzzi, 2004; Shepard, 2002; Westwood, 1994).

Most educators agree that merely presenting information about skills is not enough; the learner must be active (Westwood, 1994). Hazler and Kottler (2005) stated, "Counseling skills cannot be learned through lectures and discussions alone; they must be practiced" (p. 35). It appears that some form of practicing skills is invaluable in solidifying the information learned in the classroom and improving the empathy level of students for clients (Borders and Brown, 2005; Cummings, 1992). The most effective graduate programs in counseling, as described by Corey, Corey and Callanan (2003), are those that combine academic and personal learning as well as didactic and experiential approaches. Such programs should also include detailed and specific feedback to students about how they function with clients. These assessments are most effective when faculty review live or taped sessions by the counselors-in-training.

CURRENT METHODS OF SKILL BUILDING: PITFALLS AND PROBLEMS

One of the most commonly used methods of teaching students counseling skills is to have them practice with one another inside and outside of the classroom (i.e., role-playing). A convenient manner is to create student dyads, where each student role plays a client and then a counselor (Davis, 2003), oftentimes taping the mock sessions. Such tapes can then be evaluated by faculty. However, there are a number of potential problems with such approaches. First, some students may conduct "practice sessions" before the actual session is taped, resulting in a tape that is an inaccurate representation of their skills. Other students may prepare "scripts" which have been rehearsed prior to taping. A third problem with these mock sessions is that students may either make the session easier for one another by presenting a problem that is not challenging or by talking incessantly so that the counselor-in-training does not have to intervene often.

From a learning perspective, perhaps the greatest difficulty with students working with fellow classmates is that they often report that the situation is not "real," therefore much of their anxiety about working with actual clients remains and is not adequately addressed. They continue to express concerns about how to assist their clients, especially since working with clients can be an anxiety provoking and frightening experience for students (Meyer, Gonzalez, and Favini, 2004). These emotions may not generally be felt as intensely when the students work with one another.

PROPOSED PROGRAM

Although there is general recognition by counselor educators of the importance of using experiential activities to educate students about the counseling process (Kim and Lyons, 2003), obtaining an appropriate set of volunteer clients for counselors-in-training to practice with is difficult. Recognizing the limitations of the method of role playing to teach counseling skills, as well as desiring that the counselors-in-training have actual clients to practice their skills with, the author initiated a pilot program recruiting undergraduate volunteers from the university. In a university with a large student body, such students are available and there frequently exists an imbalance between the services that are available on college counseling centers and the number of students in need of counseling (Uffelman and Hardin, 2002). For example, on the campus on which this project took place, the counseling center served approximately 1,000 students (out of a total student body of 34,000) in one academic year (e-mail communication, Heidi VonHarschar, June 18, 2007), with a staff of 11 full time clinicians and 3 part time.

This study sought to demonstrate the effectiveness of this approach as a teaching method as well as document the successful counseling by the counselors-in-training. It was hypothesized that using "real" clients for training purposes with counselors-in-training would be rated more favorably than role-playing, which had been used in the students' introductory counseling skills course. In addition, it was hypothesized that clients would report some improvement and a positive experience with the counselors-in-training

A Teaching Model for Advanced Counseling Skills

Obtaining the Volunteers

Volunteer clients were obtained through undergraduate educational psychology courses taught by instructors other than the author. The university in which these students were enrolled is a large, urban, culturally diverse university in the southeast, classified as a minority institution. Announcements were made by the author in the classes about the nature of the project and the duration of participation. The students were informed that the author was recruiting volunteers to assist graduate counselors-in-training in practicing their counseling skills. The prospective participants were told that if they had a problem, (e.g., relationship, family, academic), they would be able to discuss these with the counselor-in-training, who would be supervised by the author. They were further informed that this was time-limited counseling and that if they continued to need help after the requisite sessions, they would be given referrals. They were also informed that the sessions would be either audio or video taped for supervision purposes, but that these tapes would be destroyed. Student volunteers submitted their names and phone numbers to the author by completing a mini-registration form, which was distributed in the classroom. They were also given the author's office phone number to call to volunteer if they did not want to sign up in class. Volunteers were informed that they might not be chosen this semester and would be placed on the list for the following semester.

During the first class meeting of the graduate counseling course, the volunteers were then randomly assigned to a counselor-in-training by the professor (author). The counselors-in-training were provided a volunteer client's name and phone number. Following the first class meeting, the counselors-in-training then contacted their clients by phone to set up the first session. If counseling students were unable to reach their volunteer, or the volunteer was no longer interested, the professor assigned another volunteer from the registration forms. This study received approval through Florida International University's Institutional Review Board for the Use of Human Subjects. For all measures described in this study, anonymity was maintained by having a research assistant compile the information contained in the questionnaires and requesting all participants to exclude any identifying information.

Volunteer Clients

Ten college undergraduates served as participants. They ranged in age from 18 to 37 ($M=24$, $SD=6.5$). Eighty percent of the participants were female, with the remaining 20% male. The participants' self-identified ethnicity was 10% Caucasian non-Hispanic, 70% Hispanic, and 20% African American. The volunteer clients presented with an array of difficulties including stress, school pressures, relationship problems, and difficulties dealing with separation from parents and family of origin issues.

Counselors-in-Training

There were 10 counselors-in-training; 8 female and 2 male. The counselors-in-training self-identified ethnicity was 20% Caucasian non-Hispanic, 60% Hispanic and 20% African American and they ranged in age from 23 to 54 ($M=36$, $SD=12.2$). The counselors-in-training were all graduate students enrolled in a CACREP accredited Master's degree program in Mental Health Counseling. Prerequisites for the current course were (at a minimum) successful completion of both (1) Counseling Skills and Techniques and (2) Personality Theories, each of which is a 3 credit course. The Counseling Skills course consists of an introduction to basic counseling theories and interviewing skills using the Ivey and Bradford Ivey (2007) microskills approach. This introductory course includes several lab exercises where students role-played with one another. In Personality Theories, students are taught a number of theories of counseling including Rogers' non-directive approach, Ellis' rational emotive behavioral therapy, Gestalt, Adlerian, and Choice therapies utilizing Corey's (2004) *Theory and Practice of Counseling and Psychotherapy*. The current course in which the graduate students were enrolled met for two hours and 40 minutes, once a week for 15 weeks.

Counseling Sessions

Clients met with their counselors for a total of 5 sessions (approximately 45 minutes each) over the course of the 15 weeks. The schedules of the undergraduate volunteers and those of the counselors-in-training necessitated a flexible approach to scheduling the sessions. Some volunteers chose to have five sessions consecutively, once a week, while others scheduled them as needed throughout the 15 week semester. The meetings took place primarily in the counseling program's clinical laboratory, located on the university campus, which is equipped with audio and video equipment. Some counseling students were employed at centers where they had a confidential office space and chose to schedule their sessions there, if the client agreed. (It should be noted that the graduate students enrolled in this counselor education program are rather non-traditional, in that the majority work full-time and attend school in the evenings).

During the first counseling session, the undergraduate volunteer signed an informed consent form which included permission for audio or video taping for supervision purposes as well as agreeing to complete an evaluation form at the end of the sessions which would be used for research purposes. The first session consisted of a psychosocial history of the client, a brief mental status exam, and an evaluation of the presenting problem. In conducting the mental status exam, counselors-in-training were aware of exclusionary criteria including: present suicidal or homicidal ideation or present participation in professional counseling (i.e., psychotherapy, psychiatric treatment). If clients were deemed inappropriate for volunteering, they were given a referral to the university counseling center. (During the semester in which this study was conducted, no volunteer client had to be referred.) During this session, clients were also explained the nature and limits of confidentiality. They were further advised that the professor was a licensed psychologist and National Certified Counselor, responsible for the performance of the counselor-in-training. They were provided with the phone number of the professor, in case they had any problems or concerns about their counselors' behavior.

The next 3 sessions focused on exploring the client's presenting problem in the context of the symptoms they were experiencing. Counselors practiced primarily client-centered counseling (Rogers, 1951), with an emphasis on reflection, unconditional positive regard, and empathy, however, they were free to utilize any theory or method of counseling previously learned. The final session consisted of counselors summarizing the sessions, discussing termination and making referrals to outside counseling agencies, if necessary. It was made clear to counselors-in-training over the semester that they could not continue to see their clients outside of the class assignment as they would not be receiving supervision and were not yet competent to practice on their own.

Feedback to the Counselors-in-Training

The graduate students were required to submit audio or video tapes from any 3 of the 5 sessions and provide a partial transcript of the sessions as well as progress notes and personal reflections on the sessions. Counselor self-report of the counseling session has been traditionally used as a report of progress with clients, but is often inaccurate. Borders and Brown (2005) state, "tapes provide access to the actual counseling session content, and so are an important complement—and contrast—to self reports and process notes" (p. 41).

Ongoing feedback and evaluation of the counselors-in-training was provided to the students in a written format, as well as verbal (in class). The professor provided written comments on the transcripts related to directions to pursue in future sessions and alternate responses to the client. By listening to the sessions, via audio or video tape, the professor could accurately assess the counselors-in-training strengths and weaknesses, and provide corrective feedback on the counselor's mastery of skills. Verbal feedback, of a generic nature, was provided in class to all counselors-in-training. Issues such as a reviewing counseling skills, general handling of client issues, and appropriate responses were discussed in class.

MEASURES

Therapy Session Evaluation. Containing 8 items from the *Therapy Session Report – Patient (TSR-P)* (Kolden, 1993) (78 items), this measure was used to measure one's satisfaction with their ability to tell his or her story, and ventilate and clarify what is most troublesome (Kolden, Strauman, Gittleman, Halverson, Heerey, and Schneider, 2000). The TSR-P involves an emotional-cognitive process of sharing thoughts and feelings and clarifying what is currently distressing and problematic to the client (Kolden, et al., 2000). Seven of 8 questions were chosen from the section of the TSR-P that deals with what the client felt he or she got out of the session (Therapeutic Realization—Unburdening) and the final question was chosen as it addressed overall progress (Session Evaluation). The items are responded to on a four point Likert scale ranging from 0 to 3, with 0 representing "not at all" and 3 indicating "a great deal".

The clients were given this instrument during the last session by their counselors-in-training and asked to complete it within one week, at their leisure. This form was returned to the professor in a sealed envelope via intercampus mail so that the counselors-in-training would not have access to it, and to encourage honest responding on the part of the volunteers.

Counselor-In-Training Rating of Counseling Experience Feedback Form. The author created a 5-item measure for the purposes of obtaining feedback from the counselors-in-training regarding their perceptions of this exercise as a learning experience. This measure was included as an exploratory measure, as it is believed that the counselors'-in-training replies can help determine whether this method of training is appropriate and to what extent adjustments may need to be made to the method (Meyer, et al., 2004). The rating form consists of five items examining the counselor's perception of the counseling experience. Three were responded to using a Likert Scale, while the remaining two items were open-ended questions aimed at gathering general feedback about the benefit of such an approach over previously used methods in class. Counselors-in-training anonymously completed this form (which took approximately 10 minutes) in the last class and submitted them to the author.

RESULTS

The volunteer clients reported that they made a considerable amount of progress ($M = 1.78$, $SD = 1.05$; where 1 = "a great deal of progress" and 2 = "considerable progress") in dealing with their problems in the 5 sessions of counseling. Items 2-8 from the *Therapy Session Evaluation* were scored highly with means ranging from 2.36 to 2.80, on a scale of 0 to 3. The clients reported getting relief from unpleasant feelings and tension, a understanding of the reasons behind their behavior and feelings, and reassurance and encouragement, as well as great confidence to deal with their problems. (See Table 1 for complete results from the *Therapy Session Evaluation*).

The results of the quantitative data from the *Counselor-In-Training Rating of Counseling Experience Feedback Form* are displayed in Table 2. The qualitative research was examined in a multistep process. Miles and Huberman (1994) recommend that researchers begin with topics based on previous research and then read through the responses to identify key patterns and illustrative examples.

Table 1. Means and Standard Deviations From Therapy Session Evaluation

N=10			
Statement	Mean	SD	Range
1. How much progress do you feel you made in dealing with your problems?[a]	1.57	.62	1-6*
2. I feel that I got help in talking about what was really troubling me.[b]	.80	.41	0-3
3. I feel that I got relief from tension or unpleasant feelings	2.61	.65	0-3
4. I feel that I got more understanding of the reasons behind my behavior and feelings.	2.52	.70	0-3
5. I feel that I got reassurance and encouragement about how I am doing.	2.70	.50	0-3
6. I feel that I got confidence to try to do things differently.	2.36	.84	0-3
7. I feel that I got more ability to feel my feelings to know what I really want.	2.59	.62	0-3
8. I feel that I got more ideas for better ways of dealing with people and problems	2.5	.60	0-3

Note [a] Scale for question 1
- A great deal of progress
- Considerable progress
- Moderate progress
- Some progress
- Didn't get anywhere
- In some ways my problem seems to have gotten worse

Note [b] Scale for questions 2-6
- 0 = None
- 1= A little
- 2= Some
- 3= A lot

Table 2. Mean, Standard Deviations, and Range for Counselor-In-Training Rating of Counseling Experience

N=10			
Statement	Mean	SD	Range
1. How well do you think you helped your client with his or her difficulties?[a]	3.60	.70	1-5
2. How much did you learn from this experience of working with a "live" client?	4.60	.52	1-5
3. How would you rate this as a learning experience compared to other forms of learning?	4.50	.71	1-5

Note[a] Scale for Questions 1-3
- Not at all
- Not much
- A little
- Quite a bit
- Very much

In this case, there was no known literature addressing counselors-in-training preference for learning methods (i.e. role play vs. live). In terms of validity, several steps were taken to enhance the dependability of the results, including the use of multiple researchers to strengthen the internal validity of the study (Merriam, 2002). To this end, two other researchers were used for multiple perspectives and experiences in the data interpretation. They were graduate research assistants in the counseling program familiar with the research base. One research assistant transcribed the participants' responses to the two items. Then a copy was provided to both the author and the other research assistant, who each dependently read through the notes and generated a list of key phrases and themes in the participants' responses. These three individuals then met to review and discuss the key phrases, generate theme names and choose representative quotes.

The responses to the two open ended questions revealed generally positive feedback about the experience. Several themes emerged in response to the question, such as, "How does working with 'live' clients compare to counseling fellow classmates?" The main themes were: rewarding/learning, challenging, and realism. The first theme of rewarding/learning was referenced in comments such as, "an interesting and rewarding experience", and "great learning experience because for me it was the first opportunity to work with an individual who's background is a complete mystery". With regard to learning while conducting their sessions, counselors-in-training indicated a focus on not making mistakes and taking it more seriously than compared to when one worked with classmates: "with the live client you are on your own, using what you've learned and understand", "it is very valuable to be able to apply what is learned in class to real life situations". The second theme that occurred for the counselors-in-training was challenging. This was portrayed in comments such as: "working with a live client is challenging, I know that I am dealing with a client, I am helping someone with a real problem as opposed to problems we make up or imagine in the classroom situations", "I have to admit at first it is very, very intimidating…", "During my first counseling class, the person tried to give a challenge but not too difficult…now with the live client, you are on your own", and "at times [this experience] was frustrating". Finally, the idea of the realism of the experience was described by many counselors-in-training: "Gave me a realistic learning experience", "the situation was more realistic [than classmates], and "counseling a live client is as close as you get to the real experience".

Few suggestions were offered by the counselors-in-training to improve the program. In response to the statement, "Please provide any other information about the experience (i.e., ways in which the experience was helpful or could have been improved)", the majority of the counselors-in-training had no suggestions. The few responses that were provided included: increasing the total number of sessions required by the counselor-in-training (e.g., "I would probably increase the number of sessions to 6. I felt I had just started making progress with my client when we had to end."), having this experience in a course prior to this one (e.g. Introduction to Counseling Skills and Techniques) and a few counselors-in-training described frustrations with their particular clients (i.e., not talkative enough, too pressed for time with schoolwork demands, etc.). In addition to the specific feedback about this aspect of the course, the formal course evaluations and student assessment of instruction (which are administered, according to university policy, on the last day of class without the professor present) were excellent. Some of the comments relevant to this assignment included, "good opportunity to work with a real client", "this course afforded me my first opportunity to counsel a client one-on-one", "excellent way to teach us counseling (hands on)", "one of the most useful and productive courses due to the hands-on practical, real life situation I could experience as a counselor with a pseudo client", and "I left the course with an abundance of gained knowledge and new experiences".

EVALUATION OF THE TEACHING METHOD

This teaching model for advanced counseling skills was evaluated in an exploratory manner through the assessments completed by the volunteer clients and feedback obtained from the counselors-in-training evaluations. Responses from counselors-in-training indicated that they learned a great deal from this experience of working with actual clients and rated the experience highly compared to other methods of training they had experienced in other counseling courses (i.e. role playing). The counselors-in-training comments indicated the value of utilizing actual clients. The counselors overwhelmingly reported the benefit of having to work with a client, both in terms of enhancing their counseling skills and learning to personally handle the emotional content of the material that was presented in the sessions. Based on the feedback from the counselors-in-training, this experience appears to be a valuable teaching method and one which provides the counselors-in-training with a realistic counseling situation in which to practice their skills.

In general, the responses from the clients' evaluations indicate an overall positive experience with the counseling provided by the counselors-in-training and a feeling as though they had been helped. On the *Therapy Session Evaluation* the highest means were obtained on the item that inquired about the client's feeling about getting "help with talking about what was troubling" to them. Clients reported generally being pleased with the experience, making progress toward their counseling goal, and getting ideas for better ways of dealing with people and problems.

PRACTICAL IMPLICATIONS

An advantage of this method over others is the use of real clients, with real-life problems and issues. This population of clients is ethnically similar to the ethnic composition of the county at large, and thus prepared students for the diversity they will encounter later on in their careers. Finally, providing the undergraduate volunteers for the counselors-in-training also removes the onus of them finding a volunteer client with whom they do not have a relationship. In some cases, both the counselors-in-training and the client expressed a desire to continue the sessions, due to the formation of a therapeutic relationship and the mutual belief that the client was being helped.

Despite the success of this program, there were some difficulties encountered. At times the counselors were unable to contact their clients, or the clients would miss the assigned meeting time or fail to return phone calls. If this happened after a few sessions, the counselor was in the precarious situation of having to begin a relationship with another client partway though the semester. The professor needs to be fair and flexible with assignment deadlines when this occurs. Another problem was that some clients volunteered as a means to "help out another student" and did not have a primary concern. In turn, the graduate counseling student would be frustrated when the client reported no problems and remain guarded or silent throughout many of the sessions. Despite these minor difficulties, this teaching method should be employed. As one graduate student explained, "When working with a 'live client', the student experiences what can and does occur in the real world such as missed appointments."

LIMITATIONS AND FUTURE RECOMMENDATIONS

This teaching method may not be possible for all faculty to implement as the recruitment of the volunteers took significant time and planning on the part of the professor (i.e., finding cooperative faculty, making presentations in classes, fielding phone calls from prospective clients). At a small college, there may not be an ample volunteer pool. With regard to concluding that the counselors-in-training helped their clients, no follow up was conducted nor was a control group used. Thus, no clear cut conclusions can be drawn regarding the contributions of the interventions that took place, versus the mere effects of the time elapsed and the spontaneous resolution of problems (Barak, 1990). The implementation of a specific measure to evaluate the counselors'-in-training skills such as empathy, summarizing, and reflecting was not employed, although feedback on these skills was provided to the counselors-in-training via written feedback on the dialogue transcripts of their taped counseling sessions. Future practice (and research) could employ criteria which focuses on the trainees' demonstration of discrete skills, or on how well the trainee conceptualizes the client's problems or more advanced skills such as timing and judgment (Goodyear and Bernard, 1998). Additionally, utilizing the entire *Therapy Interview Session Report –Patient (*Kolden, 1993) in conjunction with the *Therapy Interview Session Report-Therapist (*Kolden, 1993), could yield some interesting comparisons between client and counselor perceptions.

Some counselors-in-training had the benefit of being assigned an articulate, motivated client with a presenting problem that could be addressed reasonably in the time allotted. However, not all students were so fortunate and some had difficult, resistant clients. In this experience, counselors-in-training learned how to respond to the specific needs of their client. Thus, clearly working with a single client does not allow opportunity for practicing all types of interventions or clinical skills.

CONCLUSION

In summary, this chapter outlines a method for teaching counseling skills to advanced level counselors-in-training by providing a pool of undergraduate, volunteer clients. This allowed counselors-in-training the opportunity to practice their skills with actual clients prior to embarking on practicum and internship, and provided them with a counseling experience simulating a professional relationship. The feedback from both the clients and the counselors-in-training strongly indicate that this was a successful experience. Many of the clients reported significant assistance in dealing with their presenting problem, while most of the counselors-in-training stated they benefited from the "realness" of the experience. The difficulties in implementing this model were minimal compared to the gains reported. There appears to be distinct advantages to using this model compared to student role play when teaching advanced level counselors-in-training.

REFERENCES

Barak, A. (1990). Counselor training in empathy by a game procedure. *Counselor Education and Supervision,* 29, 171-178.

Borders, L. and Brown, L. G. (2005). *The new handbook of counseling supervision.* Alexandria, VA: Association for Counselor Education and Supervision.

Corey, G., Corey, M., and Callanan, P. (2003) *Issues and ethics in the helping professions* (6th ed). Pacific Grove, CA: Brooks/Cole.

Corey, G. (2004). *Theory and practice of counseling and psychotherapy* (7th ed.).Belmont, CA: Wadsworth.

Cummings, A. (1992). A model for teaching experiential counseling interventions to novice counselors. *Counselor Education and Supervision,* 32, 23-31.

Davis, K. (2003). Teaching a course in school-based consultation. *Counselor Education and Supervision,* 42(4), 275-285.

Goodyear, R. and Bernard, J. (1998). Clinical supervision: Lessons from the literature. *Counselor Education and Supervision,* 38(1), 6-22.

Hazler, R. and Kottler, J. (2005). The emerging professional counselor: Student dreams to professional realities (2nd ed.). Alexandria, VA: American Counseling Association.

Ivey, A. and Bradford Ivey, M. (2007) *Intentional interviewing and counseling , facilitating client development in a multicultural society* (6th ed.) Pacific Grove, CA: Brooks/Cole.

Levitov, J., Fall, K., and Jennings, M. (1999). Counselor clinical training with client-actors. *Counselor Education and Supervision,* 38, 249-259.

Kim, B. and Lyons, H. (2003). Experiential activities and multicultural counseling competence training. *Journal of Counseling and Development,* 81 (4), 400-408.

Kolden, G. (1993) Therapy Session Report – Generic Model, patient version. Madison, WI: University of Wisconsin-Madison.

Kolden, G., Strauman, T., Gittleman, M., Halverson, J., Heerey, E., and Schneider, K. (2000). The therapeutic realization scale-revised (TRS-R): Psychometric characteristics and relationship to treatment process and outcome. *Journal of Clinical Psychology, 56*(9), 1207-1220.

Merriam, S.B. (Ed.) (2002). *Qualitative research in practice: Examples for discussion and analysis.* New York: John Wiley and Sons.

Miles, M. B., and Huberman, A. M. (1994). *Qualitative data analysis: A sourcebook of new methods* (2nd ed.) Thousand Oaks, CA: Sage.

Meyer, F., Gonzalez, C., and Favini, C. (2004). Didactic psychological counseling—a real challenge. *School Psychology International,* 25, 79-91.

Osborn, C., Daninhirsch, C., and Page, B. (2003). Experiential training in group counseling: Humanistic processes in practice. *Journal of Humanistic Counseling, Education, and Development,* 42, 14-29.

Osborn, C., Dean, E., and Petruzzi, M. (2004). Use of simulated multidisciplinary treatment teams and client actors to teach case conceptualization and treatment planning skills. *Counselor Education and Supervision,* 44(2), 121-134.

Rogers, C. (1951). *Client-centered therapy.* Boston: Houghton Mifflin.

Shepard, D. (2002). Using screenwriting techniques to create realistic and ethical role plays. *Counselor Education and Supervision,* 45, 145-148.

Uffelman, R. and Hardin, S. (2002). Session limits at university counseling centers: Effects on help-seeking attitudes. *Journal of Counseling Psychology, 49*, 127-132.

Westwood, M. (1994). Use of simulation activities in developing counselor competence, *Simulation and Gaming, 25,* 99-102.

Chapter 5

SOCIAL STORIES AS A SOCIAL SKILLS INTERVENTION FOR CHILDREN WITH AUTISM

Emily A. Iobst[1], Laura A. Nabors, and Meghan E. McGrady
Department of Psychology, University of Cincinnati, OH, USA

ABSTRACT

This chapter outlines the theoretical background behind the social deficits evidenced in individuals with autism. Typical social interventions directed at improving social interaction for individuals with autism are discussed, and a newer intervention, the social story intervention, is discussed in detail. Research has shown that individuals with autism have an impaired or absent theory of mind – that is, they are typically unable to infer other people's thoughts and intentions from the social environment. The social story intervention intends to supply this information to the individual with autism in an individualized format in order to reduce targeted problem behavior or encourage appropriate behavior. Research, relying predominantly on case studies, has demonstrated that the social story intervention is, for the most part, moderately to highly effective in promoting appropriate social behavior. However, the research studies investigating this intervention have methodological weaknesses that must be remedied in future research, in order to make conclusive decisions regarding the effectiveness of the social story as an intervention.

Autism has recently become a topic of intensified interest in both the field of psychology and in the popular media. In the first sections of this chapter, a review of the diagnosis of autism, prevalence of the disorder, and social deficits for children with autism is presented. A discussion of "theory of mind," a major theory advanced to explain the social deficits characterized in autism, will follow this general introduction. Next, the social story intervention is reviewed and a review of the extant literature utilizing this intervention is

---

[1] Correspondent: Emily Iobst, Mail Location 376, Department of Psychology, University of Cincinnati, Cincinnati, Ohio 45221-0376, email iobstea@email.uc.edu.

presented. The chapter concludes with a discussion of the benefits of social stories and directions for future research intended to examine the effectiveness of this intervention.

DIAGNOSTIC CRITERIA FOR AUTISTIC DISORDER

According to criteria from the *Diagnostic and Statistical Manual of Mental Disorders-Fourth Edition-Text Revision* (*DSM-IV-TR*), Autistic Disorder manifests in three behavioral categories: problems with social interaction, difficulties with verbal and nonverbal communication, and restricted repetitive, stereotyped patterns of behaviors, interests, and activities (APA, 2000). According to the *DSM-IV-TR*, an individual must exhibit two of the four following items to meet criteria for qualitative impairment in social interaction: marked impairment in the use of several nonverbal behaviors (e.g., eye-to-eye gaze, facial expression); failure to develop appropriate relationships with peers considering one's developmental level; a lack of desire to share enjoyment, interests, or achievements with others in a spontaneous manner; or a lack of social or emotional reciprocity.

Under the category of qualitative impairments in communication, at least one item from the following list must be endorsed: a delay, or absence of the development of spoken language; in those individuals who demonstrate adequate speech, a marked impairment in the ability to begin or maintain conversation with others; stereotyped and repetitive use of language or idiosyncratic language; or a lack of varied, spontaneous make-believe play or social imitative play appropriate to the child's developmental level (APA, 2000). Finally, under the restricted repetitive and stereotyped patterns of behavior, interests, or activities category, an individual must demonstrate one of the following: preoccupation with one or more stereotyped and restricted patterns of interest that is abnormal either in intensity or focus; inflexibility to specific, nonfunctional routines or rituals; stereotyped and repetitive motor behaviors; or persistent preoccupation with objects or parts of objects. In addition, the individual must show delays or abnormal functioning in at least one of the following areas, prior to the age of three: social interaction, language as used in the form of social communication, or symbolic and imaginative play (APA, 2000).

PREVALENCE OF AUTISTIC DISORDER

Estimates of the prevalence of the disorder vary. For example, Chakrabarti and Fombonne (2001) found that about 16 out of every 10,000 children had the disorder in a British sample. Yeargin-Allsopp and colleagues (2003) reported that 34 per 10,000 children had the disorder in a sample from Georgia, suggesting that there are roughly 425,000 children with autism in the United States. Differences in prevalence rates may occur as a result of variations in diagnostic practices in different areas. Specifically, it may be that children who have less severe symptoms are being diagnosed with autistic disorder in only some regions, resulting in differences in case findings (Fombonne, 2003).

Research findings also indicate a significant sex difference in the prevalence of autism. It is estimated that three to four times more boys exhibit the disorder than girls (Lovaas and Smith, 2003). For individuals with IQs in the normal range, it is estimated that males are nine times as likely to have autism as females (Wing, 1981). However, more recent estimates place the sex ratio at approximately 5:1 (Keen and Ward, 2004). Lord, Schopler, and Revicki (1982) found that although autism affects more boys than girls (a ratio of 4:1), girls who have autism tend to be more cognitively impaired than boys.

SOCIAL DEFICITS FOR CHILDREN WITH AUTISM

Arguably, the most disabling and difficult characteristic of autism is the child's lack of socialization. Although parents typically notice the failure in language development first, the deficits in language are usually preceded by social delays such as failure to make eye contact, failure to engage in social games of early infancy, a preference for inanimate objects rather than the social environment, and a relative failure to make a secure attachment to parents. In addition, the human face seems to be non-salient and holds little interest to the autistic child. Volkmar and Klin (1993) indicate that while some social skills do develop in individuals with autism, these are invariably "highly deviant, and both quantitatively and qualitatively abnormal, even in the highest-functioning individuals" (p. 43). Their difficulties with using communication to socialize with others and displaying empathy lead to failures in social interaction and isolation (Sigman and Ruskin, 1999). By the age of five, however, children with autism usually show differential social responsiveness to familiar adults, although the quality of these interactions is not typical. Social skills continue to develop as the autistic child enters late childhood and adolescence. However, even for higher-functioning children with autism, social responsivity remains an area of developmental delay.

"THEORY OF MIND" AND CHILDREN WITH AUTISM

Numerous theories have examined why a child with autism might be unable to accurately gauge information from his or her social environment and interact appropriately in it. One of the major theories in this area is that of "theory of mind." Having a theory of mind is "being able to infer the full range of mental states (beliefs, desires, intentions, imagination, emotions, etc.) that cause action. In brief, to be able to reflect on the contents of one's own and others' minds" (Baron-Cohen, 2000, p. 3). According to theory of mind, we construe people in terms of internal mental states (Wellman, 1993). In fact, our everyday interactions with other people are dependent on the understanding of others' intentions, wants, beliefs, and emotions. If we did not have a theory of mind, our social interactions would be drastically different. Children with autism may fail to develop a normal understanding that other people have minds and mental states, and that mental states relate to behavior. Research supports the idea that children with autism have difficulty understanding the perspectives, emotions, and reactions of others (Baron-Cohen, 2000; Baron-Cohen et al., 1994). People with autism also experience difficulties comprehending nonverbal communication, such as posturing, eye contact, facial affect, and tone of voice, and they often exhibit marked deficits in pragmatics or the social use of language for communication (Baron-Cohen, 1993). These types of deficits might account for the deviations these children demonstrate in social interactions and communication (Baron-Cohen, 1993).

SOCIAL STORIES AS AN INTERVENTION FOR CHILDREN WITH AUTISM

Based on the aforementioned theory, Carol Gray and her colleague designed social stories in the 1990's to help individuals with autism infer what other people might be thinking or feeling and to teach specific social skills to replace less appropriate behaviors or destructive behaviors (Gray, 1995; Gray, 1998; Gray and Garand, 1993). Social stories are designed to provide individuals with autism information about their social environments and others' thoughts and expectations of them. By providing individuals with autism information indicating what is expected of them (in the form of a story), the information that they might not have been able to infer from the social environment is available to them.

According to Gray, an effective social story includes six elements (Gray, 1995; Gray, 1998). The first element involves determining a topic. Topics are often formulated in response to difficult or distressing events or as a result of situations that have caused confusion or fear for the child with autism. The second element requires gathering information regarding the student and situation through observation of the situation and interviews with relevant individuals. Necessary information includes relevant cues, the typical sequence of events, ideas from those involved in the situation, and the perspective of the student regarding the situation. Third, Gray suggests writing guidelines to ensure that the material in the story is appropriate for addressing the targeted behaviors as well as the learning style and preferences of the child. For example, the stories must take into account the learning characteristics of the student, which helps to ensure that the child with autism will accept the quality of the social stories.

The fourth element requires that the story adhere to the Social Story Ratio. The Social Story ratio dictates that for every directive or control sentence there should be no more than 2 to 5 descriptive and/or perspective sentences. In social stories, *descriptive* sentences objectively define where a situation occurs, who is involved, what they are doing, and why. *Perspective* sentences are statements that describe a person's internal states. *Directive* sentences are statements that directly define what is expected as a response to a give cue or situation; these statements direct the student's behavior. Finally, *control* sentences are statements typically written by the targeted student to identify strategies that he/she may use to recall the information in a social story, reassure him/herself, or define his/her own response. Control sentences provide an opportunity for the student to control his/her own response by identifying meaningful, personal strategies to handle difficult situations (Gray, 1995; Gray, 1998).

Fifth, it is important to incorporate student interests into a social story. The child's interests and preferences directly influence the content, writing style, illustrations, format, or implementation of a social story. As a result, the incorporation of relevant interests may increase the child's motivation to attend to the social story. Sixth, introducing, reviewing, and monitoring a social story is the shared responsibility of all individuals working with the student. This includes teachers and parents. This can help ensure that the behaviors stressed in the intervention generalize to different settings during interactions with different people. However, this requirement is often difficult to attain because it requires that teachers, parents, and psychologists agree upon the intervention implementation and, more importantly, follow through with the implementation (Gray, 1995; Gray, 1998).

The following is a description of a social story intervention implemented by one of the authors of this chapter. Edward, a 6-year-old child diagnosed with Autistic Disorder, was in first grade at a public elementary school and spent the entire day in the Special Needs classroom with approximately eight other special needs children. Of the inappropriate behaviors that Edward exhibited, several were especially problematic. For example, when Edward did not want to do work or felt uncomfortable with a class activity, he would frequently lie on the floor. Because he was a large child and was overweight, it would typically require two adults to get him up off of the floor. In addition, Edward would frequently throw temper tantrums when lying on the floor, and when angered he could flail his arms and legs and potentially harm others in the classroom. He had difficulty following directions and remaining seated to complete his academic work and often threw tantrums on the floor when it was time to work on his academic task. His tantrums occurred on a frequent, daily basis. Thus, the first author created a social story to address the targeted problem behavior of lying on the floor and having temper tantrums:

My name is Edward[2]. I go to Elwood Elementary School. My teacher is Mrs. Jones. In class, the students sit at their desk to do work. When they do not want to do work, the students usually tell the teacher using words. They usually do not lie on the floor. Sometimes I lay on the floor when work is not fun for me or when I do not want to do work. It's important to listen to Mrs. Jones when she gives me directions. I should sit in my seat even when I do not want to do work. I will try to stay in my seat even when I do not want to do my work or when it is not fun for me. I will try not to lie on the floor.

In developing this story, the first author followed Gray's guidelines: including the use of descriptive, directive, perspective, and control sentences; writing the story from Edward's perspective; writing the story at a level that Edward could comprehend; and incorporating Edward's interests into the story (Gray, 1995; Gray, 1998).

There are several advantages to using social stories as an intervention. For example, social stories are a relatively inexpensive method of intervening to improve the social interactions of children with autism. In addition, they can be easily individualized to meet the goals of each child. For example, clinicians can develop stories to be used by teachers, paraprofessionals, or parents, who can read the stories with the children. Journals or behavioral records can be used to document how stories are implemented and record changes in social interactions (Sansosti and Powell-Smith, 2006). This allows for data collection that will inform additional clinical interventions aimed at ameliorating other social problems or acquisition of new skills. The next section of this chapter (see Table 1) reviews research focusing on the use of social stories with children who have autism.

---

[1] Names of the child and teacher were changed for presentation in this chapter.

RESEARCH STUDIES USING SOCIAL STORIES WITH CHILDREN WITH AUTISM

Table 1. Studies using Social Stories to Improve Problem Behaviors and Social Skills

Authors	Participants	Targeted Behaviors
Adams, Gouvousis, VanLue, and Waldron (2004)	1 child with autism	challenging behaviors (hitting, crying, falling, screaming) during homework time
Brownell (2002)	4 children with autism	echolalia related to TV or movies, difficulty following instructions, using loud voice inappropriate to context
Hagiwara and Myles (1999)	3 children with autism	washing hands, on-task behavior
Ivey, Heflin, and Alberto (2004)	3 children with Pervasive Developmental Disorder	difficulties with changes in routines
Kuoch and Mirenda (2003)	3 children with autism	eating problems at school, problems during play (e.g., cheating, moving pieces of other players)
Kuttler, Myles, and Carlson (1998)	1 child diagnosed with autism	tantrum behavior
Lorimer, Simpson, Myles, and Ganz (2002)	1 child with autism	interrupting verbalizations and tantrums
Norris and Dattilo (1999)	1 child with autism	inappropriate social interaction during lunch
Rowe (1999)	1 child with Asperger's Disorder	refusal to eat lunch with other children and inappropriate peer interactions during lunchtime
Sansosti and Powell-Smith (2006)	3 children with Asperger's Disorder	behavior problems during group interactions; difficulty with social communication
Swaggart and colleagues (1995)	3 children with moderate to severe autism	appropriate greeting behavior, sharing
Thiemann and Goldstein (2001)	5 children with autism	social communication skills (e.g., contingent responses, securing attention, initiating comments, initiating requests)

The studies in Table 1 show that the use of individualized stories, addressing problem behaviors and skills deficits, were effective, at least in the short-term, in improving functioning for children with autism. The results of these studies indicated that using a simply constructed story read daily over a relatively short period of time can produce encouraging results – the social story intervention seemed to provide the participant with the information he or she was unable to infer from the social environment (Gray and Garand, 1993). There is a growing body of research addressing the effectiveness of social stories as interventions to improve children's behavioral functioning or social skills (see Sansosti, Powell-Smith, and Kincaid, 2004 for a review). The following paragraphs present an in-depth review of five studies, not presented in Table 1, examining the effectiveness of social stories in remediating behavioral problems and social skills deficits of children with autism spectrum disorders.

Crozier and Tincani (2005) used social stories to decrease teacher-identified target behavior in an 8-year-old boy with autism. Following teacher interviews, talking out, defined as instances during which the child talked to teachers or other adults without raising his hand or being called on to speak, was identified as the target behavior (i.e., behavior to change). This study used an ABAC reversal design. During the baseline phase (A), the experimenters observed the participant in the classroom to obtain a baseline rate of target behavior. During the first intervention phase (B), the child listened to a modified Social Story without verbal prompts, completed a comprehension check, and returned to the classroom. Following the presentation of six intervention sessions, the intervention was removed. After a period at baseline, the child participated in a second intervention phase (C), which included the modified Social Story and the addition of verbal prompts. In each phase, an observer collected data indicating the frequency of target behaviors during each classroom session.

As a result of the intervention, the participant decreased talking out behavior. The number of instances of talking out or "talk-outs" decreased from the baseline average of 11.2 talk-outs per 30-minute observation session to 2.3 per 30-minute observation session. After an increase to 8 per 30-minute observation session during the second baseline phase, talk-outs decreased to the lowest average across all sessions (.2 per 30-minute observation session) during the second intervention phase. These results suggested that in conjunction with Social Stories, verbal prompts might serve as effective reminders of appropriate classroom behavior. Follow-up data collected two weeks after the final intervention session, suggested that low levels of problem behavior were effectively maintained after the study had ended. Post-intervention teacher interviews indicated that all teachers viewed Social Stories favorably and reported that they would use them as interventions in their classrooms.

Delano and Snell (2006) investigated the effects of social stories on social engagement in three children (ages 6 to 9 years) with autism. The children participated in a baseline (A) and an intervention session (B) that included three activities: (1) reading, (2) reading comprehension check, and (3) free play. The baseline (A) and intervention session (B) were the same except that during the baseline phase the child heard a story from a children's book from the classroom. During the intervention phase, the child heard a social story created in accordance with the Gray's recommendations (Gray, 2000). Experimenters collected data on the duration of social behaviors after each phase ended. Social behaviors included attention seeking, initiating comments, initiating requests, and contingently responding to peers' initiations (Delano and Snell, 2006). Results indicated that all three participants increased the duration of time they spent socially engaged with other peers while in the intervention setting.

Barry and Burlew (2004) investigated the effectiveness of two types of social stories on the choice-making skills and play behaviors of two children with severe autism (7- and 8-years-old). The goal of this social story intervention was to provide a positive behavioral support that would enable these children to communicate their choice of play material and then select and play with the materials during a 30-minute free-play period. The social stories in this study were written to include descriptions of environmental and behavioral cues, descriptions of the settings in which the story took place, and photographs illustrating the behavioral skills targeted in the intervention. An ABCD design was utilized in which (A) was the baseline phase, (B) was a teacher-led instructional phase in which two social stories, one on choice making and one on appropriate play in learning centers, were introduced, (C) was a teacher-led instructional phase in which a third social story was introduced, which focused on appropriate play with peers, and (D) was a phase in which the social stories were available but teacher help was not. To collect data on choice making, teachers and their assistants recorded the amount of prompting children needed to make a decision. Appropriate play was defined as interacting with the materials and/or peers in the same ways as peers who were typically developing. Teachers and their assistants recorded the duration of appropriate play for each child. The social stories were read daily in phases B and C, and the teachers also prompted children to practice the behaviors described in the stories. Corrective feedback also was given during phases B and C to improve the children's interactions. In phase D, the social stories were read each day, but the teachers did not provide corrective feedback about the children's behaviors.

The results of this study (Barry and Burlew, 2004) indicated that both children made significant gains in choice making without prompting over the 21 days of the study. At baseline, neither child was able to make independent choices about play materials or demonstrate appropriate play. Children had improved by the end of phase D. The authors concluded that one of the children was able to make choices without any prompting and the other child was able to make choices with minimal prompting when the intervention was completed. In terms of exhibiting appropriate play behaviors with peers, one child was able to increase the duration of appropriate play by 25 minutes, while the other child was able to increases the duration by 10 minutes.

Bledsoe, Myles, and Simpson (2003) utilized a social story intervention with an adolescent with Asperger's Disorder. The child's targeted behaviors were eating-related problems that resulted in peer avoidance (e.g., talking with his mouth full, failing to wipe food off of his face, spilling food and drink on both the table and his clothing). The goal of the social story intervention was to help the child improve his eating habits because it "appeared that the participant lacked an understanding of basic etiquette and eating skills, including the social implications of poor skills" (p. 291). An ABAB design was implemented: (A) baseline information was gathered for 7 days, (B) the social story was read to the adolescent for 5 days prior to lunch, (A) baseline information was gathered for 5 days, and (B) the social story was reintroduced for 4 days. The measured behaviors included spilling and wiping, and were assessed daily at lunchtime. For spilling, the median behavior frequency was 4 at baseline, 2 during the first intervention phase, 3 during the return to baseline, and 1 during the second intervention phase. For face wiping, the median behavior frequency was 0 during baseline, 1 during the first intervention phase, 0 during the return to baseline, and 1 during the second intervention phase. Consequently, there was a slight increase in positive behaviors and a slight decrease in undesirable behaviors following the implementation of the social story intervention.

Scattone, Wilczynski, Edwards, and Rabian (2002) used a social story intervention with three children with autism. Participants were between the ages of 7 and 15 years. Child One's targeted behavior was tipping his chair backward or sideways, which would often result in his chair falling over. The target behavior for Child Two was staring inappropriately at females during recess. This behavior was chosen because it often disrupted the activities of other students. Child Three's targeted behavior was shouting during his teacher's lessons. Three child-specific social stories were developed to improve each participant's disruptive behaviors, such that Child One's story described why he should not tip his chair, Child Two's story explained that he should only look at girls for two seconds and then look at something else, and Child Three's story described why he should not "holler" during class. Researchers utilized a multiple baseline design (ABAB design) to assess behavior change for each child. Behavior was assessed over 22 sessions. Graduate and undergraduate research assistants recorded baseline data about the frequency of targeted behaviors and measured the same behaviors during the intervention phase. Targeted behaviors were recorded in 20-minute observations approximately three times per week. For Child One, data were collected during large group activities, for Child Two data were collected at recess, and for Child Three, data were collected during math class. In the intervention phase, the children read or were read their social stories once a day by their teacher or a teacher's aide.

At baseline (Scattone et al., 2002), Child One's chair tipping was exhibited during 48% to 60% of the observation intervals and decreased to an average of 17% during the intervention phase. For Child Two, baseline data indicated staring occurred during an average of 66.9% of the observation intervals and was reduced to an average of 18.3% during the intervention phase. Shouting occurred for Child Three an average of 16% during the observation intervals and occurred only 5.1% of the time during the intervention. Consequently, these researchers reported that the social stories were effective in reducing the targeted behavior for each of the children (Scattone et al., 2002). These researchers felt that the effectiveness of using social stories with their participants was noteworthy because social stories are "convenient, are unobtrusive, and may draw on a strength many children with autism demonstrate (i.e., adherence to rules/routines)" (p. 540).

CONCLUSION

The research reviewed in this chapter outlines the uses and benefits of using social stories to improve problematic classroom behaviors of children with autism. Advantages of the social story intervention are that this technique is an individualized intervention, easy to implement, and often results in short-term success in improving social behaviors. In the future, conducting larger scale studies and examining the effectiveness of social stories for children with different levels of cognitive impairment will yield more information about the utility of this intervention. The premise behind the development of this intervention was at least in part based on the notion that individuals with autism do not have a fully functional theory of mind. As a result, social information must be explicitly provided to them in order to ensure appropriate social interaction. A social story is a method for providing guidance that is appealing to the individual with autism, as it reduces the social demands involved in learning a new skill (Sansosti and Powell-Smith, 2006).

In order to increase the validity of the social story intervention for it to be rightfully included in the armamentarium of successful interventions used to ameliorate the social skills deficits of children with autism, several issues must be addressed. First, research with greater experimental control should be conducted comparing the social story intervention to other interventions and including a greater number of participants. Second, research should be directed at determining the level of intelligence necessary for children to be able to respond to and benefit from this intervention. For example, researchers need to conduct studies with larger sample sizes and assess cognitive functioning of all study participants to determine if the stories are a useful intervention for those with cognitive skills that are below average in comparison to children in their age range. Third, the generalization of the social story intervention across behaviors and settings must be tested. Fourth, the long-term effects of the social story intervention should be examined to determine if the use of this intervention produces lasting change in the children's social skills.

REFERENCES

Adams, L., Gouvousis, A., VanLue, M., and Waldron, C. (2004). Social story intervention: Improving communication skills in a child with autism spectrum disorder. *Focus on Autism and Other Developmental Disabilities, 19*, 87-94.

American Psychiatric Association (2000). *Diagnostic and statistical manual of mental disorders-text revision (DSM-IV-TR)* (4th Ed.). Washington D.C.: Author.

Baron-Cohen, S. (1993). From attention-goal psychology to belief-desire psychology: The development of a theory of mind, and its dysfunction. In S. Baron-Cohen, H. Tager-Flusberg, and D. J. Cohen (Eds.), *Understanding other minds: Perspectives from autism* (pp. 59-82). New York: Oxford University.

Baron-Cohen, S. (2000). Theory of mind and autism: A fifteen year review. In S. Baron-Cohen, H. Tager-Flusberg, and D. J. Cohen (Eds.), *Understanding other minds: Perspectives from developmental cognitive neuroscience* (2nd ed.). (pp. 1-20). New York: Oxford University.

Baron-Cohen, S., Ring, H., Moriarty, J., Shmitz, P., Costa, D., and Ell, P. (1994). Recognition of mental state terms: A clinical study of autism, and a functional neuroimaging study of normal adults. *British Journal of Psychiatry, 165*, 640-649.

Barry, L. M., and Burlew, S. B. (2004). Using social stories to teach choice and play skills to children with autism. *Focus on Autism and Other Developmental Disabilities, 19*, 45-51.

Bledsoe, R., Myles, B. S., and Simpson, R. L. (2003). Use of social story intervention to improve mealtime skills of an adolescent with Asperger syndrome. *Autism, 7*, 289-295.

Brownell, M. D. (2002). Musically adapted social stories to modify behaviors in students with autism: Four case studies. *Journal of Music Therapy, 39*, 117-144.

Chakrabarti, S., and Fombonne, E. (2001). Pervasive developmental disorders in preschool children. *Journal of the American Medical Association, 285*, 3093-3099.

Crozier, S., and Tincani, M. J. (2005). Using a modified social story to decrease disruptive behavior of a child with autism. *Focus on Autism and Other Developmental Disabilities, 20*, 150-157.

Delano, M., and Snell, M. E. (2006). The effects of social stories on the social engagement of children with autism. *Journal of Positive Behavior Interventions, 8*, 29-42.

Fombonne, E. (2003). The prevalence of autism. *Journal of the American Medical Association, 289*, 87-89.

Gray, C. (2000). *The new social story book*. Arlington, TX: Future Horizons.

Gray, C. A. (1995). Teaching children with autism to read social situations. In K. A. Quill (Ed.), *Teaching children with autism* (pp. 219-241). New York: Delmar.

Gray, C. A. (1998). Social stories and comic strip conversations with students with Asperger syndrome and high-functioning autism. In E. Schopler, G. B. Mesibov, and L. J. Kunce (Eds.), *Asperger syndrome or high-functioning autism?* (pp. 167-198). New York: Plenum.

Gray, C. A., and Garand, J. D. (1993). Social stories: Improving responses of students with autism with accurate social information. *Focus on Autistic Behavior, 8*, 1-10.

Hagiwara, T., and Myles, B. S. (1999). A multimedia social story intervention: Teaching skills to children with autism. *Focus on Autism and Other Developmental Disabilities, 14*, 82-95.

Ivey, M. L., Heflin, L. J., and Alberto, P. (2004). The use of social stories to promote independent behaviors in novel events for children with PDD-NOS. *Focus on Autism and Other Developmental Disabilities, 19*, 164-176.

Keen, D., and Ward, S. (2004). Autistic spectrum disorder: A child population profile. *Autism, 8*, 39-48.

Kuoch, H., and Mirenda, P. (2003). Social story interventions for young children with autism spectrum disorders. *Focus on Autism and Other Developmental Disabilities, 18*, 219-227.

Kuttler, S., Myles, B. S., and Carlson, J. K. (1998). The use of social stories to reduce precursors to tantrum behavior in a student with autism. *Focus on Autism and Other Developmental Disabilities, 13*, 176-182.

Lord, C., Schopler, E., and Revicki, D. (1982). Sex differences in autism. *Journal of Autism and Developmental Disorders, 12*, 317-330.

Lorimer, P. A., Simpson, R. L., Myles B. S., and Ganz, J. B. (2002). The use of social stores as a preventative behavioral intervention in a home setting with a child with autism. *Journal of Positive Behavior Interventions, 4*, 53-60.

Lovaas, O. I., and Smith, T. (2003). Early and intensive behavioral intervention in autism. In A. E. Kazdin and J. R. Weisz (Eds.), *Evidence-based psychotherapies for children and adolescents* (pp. 325-340). New York: Guilford.

Norris, C., and Dattilo, J. (1999). Evaluating effects of a social story intervention on a young girl with autism. *Focus on Autism and Other Developmental Disabilities, 14*, 180-186.

Rowe, C. (1999). Do social stories benefit children with autism in mainstream primary schools? *British Journal of Special Education, 26*, 12-14.

Sansosti, F. J., and Powell-Smith, K. A. (2006). Using social stories to improve the social behavior of children with Asperger Syndrome. *Journal of Positive Behavior Interventions, 8*, 43-57.

Sansosti, F. J., Powell-Smith, K. A., and Kincaid, D. (2004). A research synthesis of social story interventions for children with autism spectrum disorders. *Focus on Autism and Other Developmental Disabilities, 19*, 194-204.

Scattone, D., Wilczynski, S. M., Edwards, R. P., and Rabian, B. (2002). Decreasing disruptive behaviors of children with autism using social stories. *Journal of Autism and Developmental Disabilities, 32*, 535-543.

Sigman, M., and Ruskin, E. (1999). Continuity and change in the social competence of children with autism, Down syndrome, and developmental delays. *Monographs of the Society for Research in Child Development, 64*, v-114.

Swaggart, B. L., Gagnon, E., Bock, S. J., Earles, T. L., Quinn, C., Myles, B. S., et al. (1995). Using social stores to teach social and behavioral skills to children with autism. *Focus on Autistic Behavior, 10*, 1-15.

Thiemann, K. S., and Goldstein, H. (2001). Social stories, written text cues, and video feedback: Effects on social communication of children with autism. *Journal of Applied Behavior Analysis, 34*, 425-446.

Volkmar, F. R., and Klin, A. (1993). Social development in autism: Historical and clinical perspectives. In S. Baron-Cohen, H. Tager-Flusberg, and D. J. Cohen (Eds.), *Understanding other minds: Perspectives from autism* (pp. 40-55). New York: Oxford University.

Wellman, H. M. (1993). Early understanding of mind: The normal case. In S. Baron-Cohen, H. Tager-Flusberg, and D. J. Cohen (Eds.), *Understanding other minds: Perspectives from autism* (pp. 10-39). New York: Oxford University.

Wing, L. (1981). Language, social, and cognitive impairments in autism and severe mental retardation. *Journal of Autism and Developmental Disorders, 11*, 31-44.

Yeargin-Allsopp, M., Rice, C., Karpurkar, T., Doernberg, N., Boyle, C., and Murphy, C. (2003). Prevalence of autism in a US metropolitan area. *Journal of the American Medical Association, 289*, 49-55.

Chapter 6

EFFECTIVE SCHOOL-BASED MENTAL HEALTH INTERVENTIONS FOR URBAN YOUTH

Dana Rofey[1], Laura Nabors[2,3], and Irina Sumajin Parkins[3]
[1]Department of Pediatrics, University of Pittsburgh, PA, USA
[2]Department of Psychology, University of Cincinnati, OH, USA
[3]Division of Behavioral Medicine and Clinical Psychology,
Cincinnati Children's Hospital Medical Center, OH, USA

ABSTRACT

Effective treatments are needed to improve mental health services for low-income, minority families. Transporting effective interventions to school-based mental health (SBMH) clinics may improve outcomes for children receiving services; however, implementation studies may be needed to measure the effectiveness of these interventions. Several programs are discussed that are empirically validated and successful in the community or in SBMH clinics. This chapter emphasizes important key components such as parental involvement, case management, children's empowerment, and mentoring to improve students' adjustment and achievement at school. Translating benefits of mental health services into gains valued by school administrators and teachers may improve acceptance of mental health services within schools. It is concluded that transporting and implementing interventions in SBMH clinics may improve children's academic, emotional and behavioral functioning and may provide valuable data for funding to ensure the growth of SBMH programs.

Longitudinal studies of inner city mental health centers indicate that the "no-show" rate for appointments is at least 50% (Sanchez-Hucles, 1999; Zahner, Pawelkiewicz, DeFrancesco, et al., 1992). The stigma attached to receiving mental health services may prevent many children from low-income, minority families from receiving treatment (U.S. Public Health Service, 2000). Moreover, African American children and families residing in

---

[3] Requests for Reprints: Laura Nabors, Mail Location 376, Department of Psychology, University of Cincinnati, Cincinnati, Ohio 45221-0376.

urban areas have reported that mental health providers need to deliver more culturally appropriate treatment (Fong and Futuro, 2001; Matt and Navarro, 1997; Wills, 1998). As our society moves toward multiculturalism, research aimed at recording what types of mental health services are most beneficial for individuals from different ethnic groups will be important (Illovsky, 2003).

Due to the lack of services for urban children from low-income families (e.g., community-based clinics often have long waiting lists), we recommend providing mental health services in schools (Nabors and Rofey, 2003). As the United States moves toward a multicultural society, more information about how interventions work for children from ethnic minority groups will be needed (Illovsky, 2003). Implementation studies are one method for examining whether successful clinic-based interventions can be effectively deployed in community settings, like school-based mental health (SBMH) clinics (Chorpita, Yim Donkervoet, et al., 2002; Connor-Smith and Weisz, 2003; Nabors and Rofey, 2003). Thus, this chapter presents information about how implementation studies can be used to examine whether interventions can be successfully transported to SBMH clinics. This chapter also will review examples of interventions that could be implemented in schools serving African American children from low-income families.

IMPLEMENTATION STUDIES

Implementation studies or fidelity checks involve assessing whether treatment was provided or delivered as planned (Moncher and Prinz, 1991). If treatment was delivered as planned and is related to enhanced outcomes, then one can assume it was successfully transported. Interventions may need to be changed or delivered differently when treatment is provided in schools (Chorpita, Yim Donkervoet, et al., 2002). Consequently, implementation studies may provide information about whether interventions need to be fine-tuned to result in optimal outcomes for children (Connor-Smith and Weisz, 2003; Schoenwald and Hoagwood, 2001).

METHODS FOR CONDUCTING IMPLEMENTATION STUDIES

Many different research techniques can be used to conduct fidelity studies (Bond, Evans, Salyers, et al., 2000; Moncher and Prinz, 1991). Videotaping sessions and then having experts code the videotapes to see what techniques were used and whether they were implemented as planned, is one way to gather information about the type of intervention that is being delivered. When the therapy treatment process implemented is associated with outcomes, research and practice can intersect, increasing knowledge about what interventions are related to successful outcomes (Bickman, 1992). Another method, that is less costly and also may provide information about the type of interventions, is using fidelity checklists to document the content of sessions (Everhard and Wandersman, 2000; Schoenwalkd, Henggeler, Bondino, et al., 2000). The fidelity checklist provides an opportunity for clinicians to record whether they implemented the interventions according to the procedures described in a manual or according to programmatic guidelines (Weersing, Weisz, Donenberg, et al., 2002).

Additionally, supervisors can review the process of treatment implementation with the clinician during supervision sessions, and then rate their perceptions of how well the clinician followed methods or adhered to the steps required for implementing interventions (Henggeler, Schoenwalkd, Liao, et al., 2002; Holloway and Neufeldt, 1995).

Unfortunately, there are drawbacks to conducting research, including implementation studies, which may challenge the utility of this strategy for deploying information in SBMH clinics. First, research can be very costly and time-consuming, and therefore difficult to conduct given the tight budgets and lack of time available in busy school clinics. Second, many clinicians and administrators may not have the expertise to conduct these studies. Third, clinicians may resist passing out consent forms and feel that these forms are detrimental to engaging children and families in treatment. Fourth, taking the time to train staff to do the research may reduce time spent in service provision (Nabors, Weist, and Reynolds, 2000). Despite these limiting conditions, research and reviews are available that have been conducted in schools and based on SBMH interventions (Greshman, Gansle, Noell, et al., 1993; Hoagwood and Erwin, 1997; Rones and Hoagwood, 2000).

An alternative to implementation studies may be to have mental health experts and community stakeholders review a mental health program to determine if it would be feasible in "their" schools and would help their students (Evans, Mullet, Weist, et al., 2006). Evans and colleagues conducted a feasibility study of this type and found that most community stakeholders and school professionals believed a mental health promotion program would help students. Evaluators endorsed the program, especially curriculum focusing on critical issues such as bullying and harassment. Improving knowledge about which interventions can be used in SBMH clinics and how they can be adapted is an important area for research (Chorpita, Yim Donkervoet, et al., 2002). References for locating other effective mental health interventions for children are presented in Table 1.

Table 1. Resources: Evidence-Based Interventions for Children

Burns, BJ, Hoagwood, K. *Community Treatment for Youth: Evidence-Based Interventions for Severe Emotional and Behavioral Disorders.* New York: Oxford University Press; 2002.

Chorpita, BF, Yim, LM, Donkervoet, JC, et al. Toward large scale implementation of empirically supported treatments for children: A review and observations by the Hawaii Empirical Basis to Services Task Force. *Clinical Psychology: Science and Practice.* 2002; 9:165-190.

Christophersen, ER, Mortweet, SL. *Treatments that Work with Children: Empirically Supported Strategies for Managing Childhood Problems.* Washington, D.C.: American Psychological Association; 2001.

Cohen, J, Fish, M. *Handbook of School-Based Interventions: Resolving Student Problems and Promoting Healthy Educational Environments.* San Francisco, CA: Jossey-Bass; 1993.

Durlak, JA. *School-Based Prevention Programs for Children and Adolescents.* Thousand Oaks, CA: Sage; 1995.

Table 1. (Continued)

Gresham, FM, Gansle, KA, Noell, GH, et al. Treatment integrity of school-based behavioral intervention studies: 1980-1990. *School Psychology Review.* 1993; 22:54-272.

Farmer, EMZ, Compton, SN, Burns, BJ, et al. Review of the evidence base for treatment of child psychopathology: Externalizing disorders. *Journal of Consulting and Clinical Psychology.* 2002; 70:1267-1302.

Hibbs, ED, Jensen, PS. *Psychosocial Treatments for Child and Adolescent Disorders: Empirically Based Strategies for Clinical Practice.* Washington, D. C.: American Psychological Association; 1996.

Hoagwood, K, Erwin, HD. Effectiveness of school-based mental health services for children: A 10-year research review. *Journal of Child and Family Studies.* 1997; 6:435-451.

Lonigan, CJ, Elbert, JC, Guest Eds. Special issue on empirically supported psychosocial interventions for children. *Journal of Clinical Child Psychology.* 1998; 27(2).

Pfeiffer, SI, Reddy, LA., Eds. *Innovative Mental Health Interventions for Children: Programs that Work.* New York, NY: Haworth Press; 2001.

Rones, M, Hoagwood, K. School-based mental health services: A research review. *Clinical Child and Family Psychology Review.* 2000; 3:223-241.

Ideas for interventions that may be deployed in SBMH clinics are presented in the next section of this chapter.

IDEAS FOR INTERVENTIONS IN SCHOOLS: "TRANSPORTABLE" TREATMENTS

Multisystemic Therapy (MST) is an effective treatment for children experiencing chronic, severe behavioral problems and for children frequenting the juvenile justice system (Henggeler, Mihalic, Rone, et al., 1998). Henggeler and colleagues have shown that their intensive intervention involving family therapy and case management services is an effective way to improve behavioral and emotional functioning for youth experiencing behavioral problems (Henggeler, Mihalic, Rone, et al., 1998; Henggeler Schoenwald, Pickrel, et al., 1994; Henggeler, Schoenwalkd, Pickrel, et al., 1995). MST has been successfully transported to a variety of community and juvenile justice settings (Schoenwald, Henggeler, Brondino, et al., 2000). This intervention strategy possesses several qualities that may make it successful in SBMH clinics. For example, MST focuses on involving the child and family members as part of the treatment team; further, clinicians treat children in the settings where problems occur and provide intensive case management services.

Several other interventions may be effective in urban schools. Atkins and colleagues have shown that the "Positive Attitudes for Learning in School" (PALS) program is effective in improving school performance and classroom behaviors (Atkins, Adil, Jackson, et al., 2001; Atkins, Frazier, Adil, et al., 2002). This intervention focuses on involving parents in their child's educational process and using peers as tutors. This program has been effective in improving children's classroom adjustment and academic performance (Atkins, Frazier, Adil, et al., 2003). The PALS program also focuses on collaboration with teachers, which is an avenue for improving children's interactions in the classroom. Another facet of this program is a focus on enhancing children's strengths. The notion of empowering individuals is a key component of successful interventions for individuals from minority groups (Matt and Navarro, 1997).

Empowering children by teaching them achievement-oriented classroom behaviors may improve their adjustment and achievement at school. This is a central tenet of Tucker's Self-Empowerment Theory (Tucker, 1999; Tucker and Herman, 2002). Tucker and her colleagues proposed that African American children from low-income families do not receive enough coaching or practice in learning achievement-oriented classroom behaviors. She has developed an after-school program that focuses on mentoring African American children so that they are empowered to learn better self-management skills and how to self-reinforce for exhibiting achievement-oriented behaviors. Tucker and her colleagues are conducting studies to examine the effectiveness of her approach (Tucker and Herman, 2002), but studies designed to test whether Tucker's program can be implemented in schools are warranted.

Many of the children referred for SBMH services may exhibit aggressive behavior or may be referred for anger management training. Lochman and his colleagues developed the "Anger Coping Program," and this program may be one that could be utilized in SBMH clinics (Lochman, Curry, Dane, et al., 2001; Lochman, Fitzgerald, and Whidby, 1999). This program was originally designed for elementary school-aged boys and is based on applying Dodge's Information Processing Model to reduce aggressive behavior. Dodge proposed that deficits in understanding peers' behaviors, interpreting what happens in social interactions, and selecting an appropriate response in different situations underlie many inappropriate or aggressive behaviors for youth with anger management and conduct problems (Lochman and Dodge, 1994).

Lochman and others initially implemented the Anger Coping Program in residential settings (Lochman, Curry, Dane, et al., 2001). This program involves group therapy in which co-therapists help children improve their perspective taking and problem solving skills (e.g., help the child improve his or her responses to problem situations and use thought to control emotions). A token system is used to reward children for participating in the sessions (Lochman, Curry, Dane, et al., 2001; Lochman, Fitzgerald, and Whidby, 1999).

OTHER INTERVENTIONS FOR PROMOTING CHILDREN'S MENTAL HEALTH

Several other interventions appear promising for promoting children's mental health. For example, Resnick et al. reported that having a supportive adult involved in the child's life was linked to positive outcomes in adolescence (Resnick, Bearman, Blum, et al., 1997).

Mentoring also may result in improved academic performance (Vance, 2002). Mentors may offer support, and therefore build resilience factors for urban youth. Mentors or supportive adults who deliver mental health promotion activities may not need professional degrees to provide effective interventions. More research assessing the effectiveness of volunteers and paraprofessionals in improving children's social and emotional functioning is needed, since this may be a cost-effective and practical way to provide more services to a greater number of children.

A relatively large body of research supports the effectiveness of mental health promotion activities delivered in the classroom for enhancing children's social and emotional functioning (Durlak, 1995; Everhart and Wandersman, 2000; Greensberg, Domitrovich, and Bumbarger, 2001; Zins, 2001). The Collaborative to Advance Social and Emotional Learning (CASEL) presented a review of evidence based mental health promotion programs (Graczyk, Matjasko, Weissberg, et al., 2000) and the CASEL website (www.casel.org) has many useful references for implementing school-based programs, especially those enhancing students social and emotional functioning. Another series of studies examining the impact of Comer's Social Development Program have shown that improving the school climate can have a positive influence on children's social and emotional functioning and academic achievement (Comer, Haynes, Joyner, et al., 2002). Experts attending a meeting convened by the World Health Organization (WHO) also suggested that the quality of the psychosocial environment is a key outcome variable for examining the effectiveness of school-based interventions (World Health Organization, 1996).

SELECTING OUTCOME INDICATORS

Positive outcomes for children receiving SBMH services may have increased practicality for school administrators if outcome variables are associated with academic achievement and positive behaviors in the classroom. Wang and others reviewed literature on promoting school success for children from urban areas (Wang and Gordon, 1994). They reported that the most important factor influencing school adjustment and academic success was the teacher's classroom management skills. The second most important factor was support from parents and family members. These two factors are rarely considered as outcome variables in research examining SBMH services.

After an intensive study of high-achieving schools in urban areas, researchers at the Dana Center in Texas presented a report detailing characteristics of high achieving schools (U.S. Department of Education, Planning and Evaluation, 1999). These included a focus on high academic standards involving all parties in the educational process (e.g., teachers, parents, and children), building interventions from students' strengths, collaborating to improve instruction in the classroom, and creating an environment that promotes and supports positive behavior. Although it is challenging to measure these broad outcome indicators, it is incumbent upon evaluators to begin to examine change in these factors for children receiving SBMH services. Translating the benefits of mental health services into gains valued by school administrators and teachers may be one of the best methods for increasing acceptance of mental health services in schools.

CONCLUSION: THE PUBLIC HEALTH PERSPECTIVE AND SBMH SERVICES

Junius Gonzales, Chief of Services Research and Clinical Epidemiology Branch at the National Institute of Mental Health, recommended using a public health approach to identify mental health interventions for community settings (Gonzalez, 2003). He suggested considering children's mental health needs as a "moving target" to be reached through a continuous process of intervention and evaluation of implementation successes and failures. If this perspective is incorporated into research on SBMH services, then implementation studies will become a critical tool for evaluating how interventions were transported to and delivered in school settings. If this process is iterative in nature, then results from research projects may inform clinical practice and serve as a mechanism to ensure that interventions are related to key outcome factors and that they positively affect the lives of children and their families (Connor-Smith and Weisz, 2003; Hawley and Weisz, 2002).

Another objective for SBMH programs will be to expand the range of services they provide, in order to increase their mental health promotion and prevention services. Mark Weist and his colleagues suggested that expanding mental health services in schools to involve mental health promotion, prevention, and early intervention services is an important step to ensure the growth of mental health services in schools (Weist, Lindsey, Moore, et al., 2006). Current and future school-based counselors are working to achieve a multi-faceted agenda involving service expansion and finding ways to introduce accountability, in terms of the effectiveness of the services that are provided, into what for many are hectic and overloaded schedules. Partnering with universities and other mental health programs to support feasibility studies (Evans, Mullett, Weist, et al., 2006) or promote the use of evidence-based practices in SBMH may be one way to improve dissemination of effective interventions. Also, team building or working collaboratively with other professionals may improve the person-power needed to address the multiple needs – in mental health promotion and intervention—for youth in schools (Brown, Dahlbeck, and Sparkman-Barnes, 2006). Team-building and offering a broad array of services may be optimal practices in urban schools where resources need to be used effectively to reach as many youth as might benefit from participating in mental health promotion, prevention, and intervention services.

It may be more cost-effective to implement evidence-based interventions in new settings, like SBMH programs, rather than develop novel interventions. Developing continuing education programs to inform school mental health clinicians about effective interventions for different childhood disorders may improve the dissemination of information and acceptance of research efforts. Funding to support dissemination efforts and fidelity studies to assess whether interventions can be deployed in SBMH clinics is needed. Successfully transporting and implementing interventions in SBMH clinics may result in improved outcomes for children receiving mental health services and provide valuable data for securing funding to ensure the viability and growth of SBMH programs. If program evaluators for SBMH programs document improved outcomes, this can lead to other opportunities for funding and service expansion to provide interventions on a broad scale, from prevention to intervention, to serve our youth.

REFERENCES

Atkins, M., Adil, J. A., Jackson, M., et al. PALS: An ecological approach to school-based mental health services in urban schools. *Report on Emotional and Behavioral Disorder in Youth, 1,* 75-77, 91-92.

Atkins, M. S., Frazier, S. L., Adil, J. A., et al. (2003). School-based mental health services in urban communities. In M. Weist, S. Evans, and N. Lever (Eds.), *Handbook of school mental health: Advancing practice and research* (pp. 165-178). New York: Kluwer Academic Publishers.

Atkins, M. S., Frazier, S. L., Adil, J. A., et al. (2002). School-based mental health services in urban communities. *Journal of Behavioral Health Services and Research, 25,* 165-175.

Bickman, L. (1992). Designing outcome evaluations for children's mental health services: Improving internal validity. In L. Bickman and D. Rog (Eds.), *Evaluating mental health services for children: New directions for program evaluation* (pp.57-68). San Francisco, CA: Jossey-Bass.

Bond, G. R., Evans, L., Salyers, M. P., et al. (2000). Measurement of fidelity in psychiatric rehabilitation. *Mental Health Services Research, 2,* 75-87.

Brown, C. B., Dahlbeck, D. T., and Sparkman-Barnes, L. (2006). Collaborative relationships: School counselors and non-school mental health professionals working together to improve mental health needs of students. *Professional School Counseling, 9,* 332-335.

Burns, B. J., and Hoagwood, K. (2002). *Community treatment for youth: Evidence-based interventions for severe emotional and behavioral disorders.* New York: Oxford University Press.

Charles A. Dana Center, University of Texas at Austin. *Hope for Urban Education: A study of nine high-performing, high-poverty, urban elementary schools.* Washington, D.C.: U.S. Department of Education, Planning and Evaluation Service; 1999.

Chorpita, B. F., Yim, L. M., Donkervoet, J. C., et al. (2002). Toward large scale implementation of empirically supported treatments for children: A review and observations by the Hawaii Empirical Basis to Services Task Force. *Clinical Psychology: Science and Practice, 9,* 165-190.

Christophersen, E. R., and Mortweet, S. L. (2001). *Treatments that work with children: Empirically supported strategies for managing childhood problems.* Washington, DC: American Psychological Association.

Connor-Smith, J. K., and Weisz, J.R. (2003). Applying treatment outcome research in clinical practice: Techniques for adapting interventions in the real world. *Child and Adolescent Mental Health, 8,* 3-10.

Cohen, J., and Fish, M. (1993). *Handbook of school-based interventions: Resolving student problems and promoting healthy educational environments.* San Francisco, CA: Jossey-Bass.

Comer, J. P., Haynes, N. M., Joyner, E. T., et al. (Eds.). (2002). *Rallying the whole village: The Comer Process for reforming education.* New York, NY: Teachers College Press.

Durlak, J. A. (1995). *School-based prevention programs for children and adolescents.* Thousand Oaks, CA: Sage.

Evans, S. W., Mullett, E., Weist, M. D., and Franz, K. (2006). Feasibility of the MindMatters school mental health promotion program in American schools. *Journal of Youth and Adolescence, 34,* 51-58.

Everhart, K., and Wandersman, A. (2000). Applying comprehensive quality programming and empowerment evaluation to reduce implementation barriers. *Journal of Educational and Psychological Consultation, 11,* 177-191.

Farmer, E. M. Z., Compton, S. N., Burns, B. J., et al. (2002). Review of the evidence base for treatment of child psychopathology: Externalizing disorders. *Journal of Consulting and Clinical Psychology, 70,* 1267-1302.

Fong, R., and Futuro, S. (Eds.). (2001) *Culturally competent practice: Skills, interventions, and evaluations.* New York: Allyn and Bacon.

Gonzalez, J. (2003). The Application of a Public Health Model to Children's Mental Health: What does this mean and how might it benefit children and families? Plenary Address at the 16th Annual Research Conference entitled, A System of Care for Children's Mental Health: Expanding the Research Base. Tampa, FL.

Graczyk, P. A., Matjasko, J. L., Weissberg, R. P., et al. (2000). The role of the Collaborative to Advance Social and Emotional Learning (CASEL) in supporting the implementation of quality school-based prevention programs. *Journal of Educational and Psychological Consultation, 11,* 3-6.

Greenberg, M. T., Domitrovich, C., and Bumbarger, B. (2001). The prevention of mental disorders in school-aged children: Current state of the field. *Prevention and Treatment, 4,* 1-19.

Gresham, F. M., Gansle, K. A., Noell, G. H., et al. (1993). Treatment integrity of school-based behavioral intervention studies: 1980-1990. *School Psychology Review, 22,* 54-272.

Hawley, K. M., and Weisz, J. R. (2002). Increasing the relevance of evidence-based treatment review to practitioners and consumers. *Clinical Psychology: Science and practice, 9,* 225-230.

Hibbs, E. D., and Jensen, P. S. (1996). *Psychosocial treatments for child and adolescent disorders: Empirically based strategies for clinical practice.* Washington, DC: American Psychological Association.

Henggeler, S. W., Mihalic, S. F., Rone, L., et al. (1998). *Blueprints for violence prevention: Multisystemic therapy.* Denver, CO: CandM Press.

Henggeler, S., Schoenwald, S., and Pickrel, S. (1995). Multisystemic Therapy: Bridging the gap between university- and community-based treatment. *Journal of Consulting and Clinical Psychology, 63,* 709-717.

Henggeler, S. W., Schoenwald, S. K., Liao, J. G., et al. Transporting efficacious treatments to field settings: The link between supervisory practices and therapist fidelity in MST Programs. *Journal of Clinical Child and Adolescent Psychology, 31,* 155-167.

Henggeler, S. W., Schoenwald, S. K., Pickrel, S. G., et al. (1994). The contribution of treatment outcome research to the reform of children's mental health services: Multisystemic therapy as an example. *Journal of Mental Health Administration, 21,* 229-239.

Holloway, E. L., and Neufeldt, S. A. (1995). Supervision: Its contribution to treatment efficacy. *Journal of Consulting and Clinical Psychology, 63,* 207-213.

Hoagwood, K., and Erwin, H. D. (1997). Effectiveness of school-based mental health services for children: A 10-year research review. *Journal of Child and Family Studies, 6,* 435-451.

Illovsky, M. E. (2003). *Mental health professionals, minorities, and the poor.* New York: Brunner-Routledge.

Lochman, J. E., Curry, J. F., Dane, H., et al. (2001). The anger coping program: An empirically-supported treatment for aggressive children. In S. Pfeiffer and L. Reddy (Eds.), *Innovative mental health interventions for children: Programs that work* (pp. 63-73). New York, NY: The Haxworth Press, Inc.

Lochman, J. E., and Dodge, K. A. (1994). Social-cognitive processes of severely violent, moderately aggressive, and nonaggressive boys. *Journal of Consulting and Clinical Psychology, 62,* 366-374.

Lochman, J. E., Fitzgerald, D. P., and Whidby, J. M. (301-349). Anger management with aggressive children. In C. Schaefer (Ed.), *Short-term psychotherapy groups for children* (pp. 301-349). Northvale, NJ: Jason Aronson Inc.

Lonigan, C. J., Elbert, J. C. (Guest Eds.). Special issue on empirically supported psychosocial interventions for children. *Journal of Clinical Child Psychology, 27(2).*

Matt, G. E., and Navarro, A. M. (1997). What meta-analyses have and have not taught us about psychotherapy effects: A review and future directions. *Clinical Psychology Review, 17,* 1-32.

Moncher, F. J., and Prinz, R. J. (1991). Treatment fidelity in outcome studies. *Clinical Psychology Review, 11,* 247-266.

Nabors, L. A., and Rofey, D. L. (2003, June). *Effectiveness and fidelity: School mental health services for at-risk youth.* Paper presented at the annual meeting of the Child Mental Health Institute, Tampa, FL.

Nabors, L. A., Weist, M. D., and Reynolds, M. W. (2000). Outcome evaluation in school mental health: Overcoming challenges and developing a research agenda. *Journal of School Health, 70,* 206-209.

Pfeiffer, S. I., and Reddy, L. A. (Eds.). (2001). *Innovative mental health interventions for children: Programs that work.* New York, NY: Haworth Press.

Resnick, M. D., Bearman, P. S., Blum, R. W., et al. (1997). Protecting adolescents from harm: Findings from the national longitudinal study on adolescent health. *Journal of the American Medical Association, 278,* 823-832.

Rones, M., and Hoagwood, K. (2000). School-based mental health services: A research review. *Clinical Child and Family Psychology Review, 3,* 223-241.

Sanchez-Hucles, J. (1999). *The first session with African Americans: A step-by-step guide.* New York: Jossey-Bass.

Schoenwald, S. K., Henggeler, S. W., Brondino, M. J., et al. Multisystemic therapy: Monitoring treatment fidelity. *Family Process, 39,* 83-103.

Schoenwald, S. K., and Hoagwood, K. (2001). Effectiveness, transportability, and dissemination of interventions: What matters when? *Psychiatric Services, 52,* 1190-1197.

Tucker, C. M. (1999). *African American children: A self-empowerment approach to modifying behavior problems and preventing academic failure.* Boston, MA: Allyn and Bacon.

Tucker, C. M., and Herman, K. C. (2002). Using culturally sensitive theories and research to meet the academic needs of low-income African American children. *American Psychologist, 57,* 762-773.

U.S. Department of Education, Planning and Evaluation Service (1999). *Hope for Urban Education: A study of nine high-performing, high-poverty, urban elementary schools.* Report by the Charles A. Dana Center, University of Texas at Austin. Washington, D.C.: Department of Education, Planning and Evaluation Service.

U. S. Public Health Service. (2000). *Report of the surgeon general's conference on children's mental health: A national action agenda.* Washington, DC.

Vance, J. E. (2002). Mentoring to facilitate resiliency in high-risk youth. In B. Burns and K. Hoagwood (Eds.), *Community treatment for youth: Evidence-based interventions for severe emotional and behavioral disorders* (pp. 139-153). New York: Oxford University Press.

Wang, M. C., and Gordon, E. W. (1994). *Educational resilience in inner-city America: Challenges and prospects.* Hillsdale, NJ: Lawrence Erlbaum Associates.

Weersing, V. R., Weisz, J. R., and Donenberg, G. R. Development of the Therapy Procedures Checklist: A therapist-report measure of technique use in child and adolescent treatment. *Journal of Clinical Child and Adolescent Psychology, 31,* 168-180.

Weist, M. D, Lindsey, M., Moore, E., and Slade, E. (2006). Building capacity in school mental health. *International Journal of Mental Health Promotion, 8,* 30-36.

Wills, W. (1998). Families with African-American roots. In E. W. Lynch and M. J. Hanson (Eds.), *Developing cross-cultural competence* (pp. 165-207). Baltimore, MD: Paul H. Brookes Publishing.

World Health Organization. (1996). *Research to improve implementation and effectiveness of school health programs.* Geneva, Switzerland.

Zahner, G. P., Pawelkiewicz, W., DeFrancesco, J. J., et al. (1992). Children's mental health service needs and utilization patterns in an urban community: An epidemiological assessment. *Journal of American Academy of Child and Adolescent Psychiatry, 31,* 951-960.

Zins, J. E. (2001). Examining opportunities and challenges for school-based prevention and promotion: Social and emotional learning as an exemplar. *Journal of Primary Prevention, 21,* 441-446.

Burns, BJ, Hoagwood, K. *Community Treatment for Youth: Evidence-Based Interventions for Severe Emotional and Behavioral Disorders.* New York: Oxford University Press; 2002.

Chorpita, BF, Yim, LM, Donkervoet, JC, et al. Toward large scale implementation of empirically supported treatments for children: A review and observations by the Hawaii Empirical Basis to Services Task Force. *Clinical Psychology: Science and Practice.* 2002; 9:165-190.

Christophersen, ER, Mortweet, SL. *Treatments that Work with Children: Empirically Supported Strategies for Managing Childhood Problems.* Washington, D.C.: American Psychological Association; 2001.

Cohen, J, Fish, M. *Handbook of School-Based Interventions: Resolving Student Problems and Promoting Healthy Educational Environments.* San Francisco, CA: Jossey-Bass; 1993.

Durlak, JA. *School-Based Prevention Programs for Children and Adolescents.* Thousand Oaks, CA: Sage; 1995.

Gresham, FM, Gansle, KA, Noell, GH, et al. Treatment integrity of school-based behavioral intervention studies: 1980-1990. *School Psychology Review.*1993; 22:54-272.

Farmer, EMZ, Compton, SN, Burns, BJ, et al. Review of the evidence base for treatment of child psychopathology: Externalizing disorders. *Journal of Consulting and Clinical Psychology.* 2002; 70:1267-1302.

Hibbs, ED, Jensen, PS. *Psychosocial Treatments for Child and Adolescent Disorders: Empirically Based Strategies for Clinical Practice.* Washington, D. C.: American Psychological Association; 1996.

Hoagwood, K, Erwin, HD. Effectiveness of school-based mental health services for children: A 10-year research review. *Journal of Child and Family Studies.* 1997; 6:435-451.

Lonigan, CJ, Elbert, JC, Guest Eds. Special issue on empirically supported psychosocial interventions for children. *Journal of Clinical Child Psychology.* 1998; 27(2).

Pfeiffer, SI, Reddy, LA., Eds. *Innovative Mental Health Interventions for Children: Programs that Work.* New York, NY: Haworth Press; 2001.

Rones, M, Hoagwood, K. School-based mental health services: A research review. *Clinical Child and Family Psychology Review.* 2000; 3:223-241.

Chapter 7

MEN'S WAYS OF MOURNING AND THEIR IMPLICATIONS FOR PSYCHOLOGICAL COUNSELING

Nehami Baum
School of Social Work, Bar Ilan University, Israel

ABSTRACT

Based on the literature on loss and bereavement, this chapter will explore men's ways of mourning. Covering a range of losses through death (of a child, parent, spouse) and other events (divorce, immigration, wife's miscarriage), the chapter will discuss when, how, and what men mourn, in distinction from women. The chapter will argue that full recognition of men's losses in these instances, especially losses through non-death events, which tend to be disenfranchised in men, is an essential pre-requisite to offering men the emotional help they may need. It will also argue that since men mourn the losses differently from women, counselors must take their unique ways of mourning into consideration in their treatment of men. Finally, the chapter will offer practical suggestions on when and how to reach out with offers of help to men, on ways of facilitating the mourning process of men in therapy, and on issues to consider in the treatment termination with men.

INTRODUCTION

In recent years, increasing attention has been paid to the feelings and needs of men in bereavement. It is by now well understood that men may be strongly affected by the death of a close family member. Fathers who lost a newborn to death have been found to respond with crying, depression, hysteria and loneliness in the immediate aftermath (Kimble, 1991), and those who lost a baby to studiously avoid, years later, situations that would remind them of their loss (Bryant, 1989). Midlife men demonstrated strong affect following the death of their mother (Douglas, 1990-91). Stroebe and Stroebe (1983), in a review of longitudinal studies of adjustment to the death of a spouse in a variety of countries, found that men were even more prone to adverse responses, such as depression, physical ailments, death and suicide, than women. Even so, it is still widely believed that men's grief in these situations is less intense than women's (e.g., Martin and Doka, 2000).

Men's grief over non-death losses is much less recognized. For example, immigration, which takes people from a familiar homeland and friends, is recognized as a source of loss for women (Salgado de Snyder, Cervantes and Padilla, 1990), but studies of men focus on their coping give little quarter to their sense of loss (Dion and Dion, 2001).

Men's suffering as a result of their losses in divorce, especially of custody of their children and natural contact with them, is rarely dealt with in the literature. Arendell (1992) goes so far as to observe that "Men are the unrecognized emotional victims of divorce" (p.580).

The loss of a child through a wife's miscarriage is often perceived as solely the women's loss (Cecil, 1994; Neugebauer et al., 1992). Very little attention is given to the father's feelings (Abboud and Liamputtong, 2003; Oakley, McPherson and Roberts, 1990; Puddifoot and Johnson, 1999), even though pregnancy has long been recognized as an experience in which the man may participate along with the woman.

In general, men's grief following non-death losses tends to be disenfranchised. Disenfranchised grief has been defined by Doka (1989) as "grief that persons experience when they incur a loss that is not or cannot be openly acknowledged, publicly mourned, or socially supported" (pg. 4). Several indications of such disenfranchisement are found in studies of responses to miscarriage. Day and Hook (1987) report that family relatives and friends did not know what to say and how to respond to men when their wives had a miscarriage, and many of them tended to ignore the event. Puddifoot and Johnson, (1997) found that when men expressed their grief over a miscarriage to their parents, the latter reminded them that it was their wives, not they, who were suffering. Gilbert and Smart (1992) found that men received little support or sympathy at work following the miscarriage of their wife and that both their boss and colleagues expected them to recover quickly.

The disenfranchisement, Doka (1989) explains, stems from the fact that every society has norms– "mourning rules" -- that clarify who is supposed to mourn, when, where, how, and for how long. In our society, the norms tend to correspond with women's ways of mourning. As Gilbert (1996) argues in his aptly entitled article, "We've had the Same Loss, Why Don't we Have the Same Grief?" men tend to express their grief differently from the socially prescribed expectations. Cook (1988) similarly points out that the traditional image of "healthy grief" is based on "women's grief". More will be said of this shortly.

Men rarely receive the help that women do in coping with their losses. As is well known, men are much less prone than women to seek psychological help with any sort of problem. The emotional problems stemming from loss, whether through the death of a loved one (Carroll and Shaefer, 1993-1994), immigration (Walsh and Horenczyk, 2001), miscarriage (Puddifoot and Johnson, 1997), or divorce (Lehr and MacMillan, 2001) are no exception.

Men's reluctance to seek help may be understood in light of their socialization and the societal expectations of them. Male sex role socialization, with its men-must-be-strong ethos, directs men to self-sufficiency, independent problem-solving, and inhibition of feelings, and does not prepare them to seek help and support for emotional matters. It teaches that men who seek help are weak, vulnerable, and incompetent (Myers, 1989; Carverhill, 1997). Consistent with this understanding, scholars who have compared the help-seeking of men and women explain men's relative reluctance to seek help by the challenge that seeking help poses to their sense of masculinity and self esteem (Fisher, Nadler and Whitcher-Alagna, 1982) and by the relative difficulty they have in identifying, talking about and admitting their psychological and social problems (Corney, 1990; Rickwood and Braithwaite, 1994).

Men are rarely offered the emotional help that is often made available to women in similar situations. For example, Walsh and Horenczyk (2001) found that although English-speaking female immigrants to Israel were offered professional help, male immigrants were not. Puddifoot and Johnson, (1997) found that men whose wives had a miscarriage received little help or support from medical staff in hospitals in England. Gray (2001), who ran a support center for couples after a miscarriage in Montreal, reports that men repeatedly told her that health professionals ignored them, and that when they sought help they were told that the support groups were for women only. Lehr and MacMillan (2001) quote divorced men telling that when they phoned to inquire about help from community agencies in Canada, they were told in effect that the agencies "don't work with men".

Where help is offered to men, it tends to be psycho-educational in approach and to focus on enabling them to better meet the needs of others. For example, Murray, Terry, Vance, Battistutta, and Connolly, (2000) report that the help offered to men following the death of a child by the helping professionals in Australia was mostly cognitive and designed to help them to help their wives cope with the loss. Similarly, numerous scholars found that the professional help that is available to divorced men is channeled to divorced fathers and focuses on encouraging and enabling them to function as non-custodial parents (Shapiro, and Lambert, 1999).

The psycho-educational approach has its merits. It is certainly worth helping husbands to give their wives emotional support in the wake of a miscarriage and divorced fathers to improve their parenting motivation and competency. The problem is that there is little emotional help for men struggling with the pain of loss. At least part of the reason lies with the lack of understanding of men's grief on the part of clinicians who have been socialized to view grief through feminine norms and their difficulty in seeing men's distress through the anger and rage that often mask it (Martin and Doka, 2000; Myers, 1989; Stinson, Lasker, Lohmann and Toedter, 1992; Walsh and Horenczyk, 2001). It has also been suggested that clinicians perceive men to benefit less than women from emotional intervention (Hobfoll, Lerman, 1989; Meth and Pasick, 1990; Murray et al, 2000).

To provide men with the help they need, professionals must be familiar with their unique way of mourning: when they usually begin the mourning process, how they mourn their losses, and what precisely are the losses that they mourn. The next section of this chapter will discuss these issues with respect to both death and non-death losses by comparing men's ways of mourning with women's.

When

For the most part, the literature suggests that women grieve both death and non-death losses earlier than men and that men's expression of grief is delayed.

Studies that examined the impact of an infant's death on the two parents consistently found differences in the time at which mothers and fathers display their grief (Stinson et al., 1992). Mothers show their grief immediately upon the death of the infant. Fathers tend to be more reserved at this stage and to channel their distress into anger, often at the medical staff. It is only with time that feelings such as sadness, grief, and distress emerge. De Frain,

Martens, Stork and Stork (1990-91) found that while mothers experienced high levels of grief immediately after the demise and a decline after two years, fathers experienced a rise in grief two years later.

Similar gender differences were found in response to the death of an older child. Bohannon (1990) found that while women scored significantly higher than their husbands on despair, anger, guilt, social isolation, loss of control, rumination, depersonalization, somatization, death anxiety, vigor and physical strength, in the first year after the death, the men scored higher on denial. Fish (1986) found that men who lost their children were more socially isolated than women who lost their children in the first two years after the death, but that the difference declined over time, so that two years later women's isolation was greater than men's.

Studies on spousal bereavement similarly show that most women experience strong emotional distress immediately upon the death of their spouse, while men tend to feel it later and for longer. Thus, Stroebe, Stroebe, and Schut's (2001) meta analysis of dozens of studies of gender differences in responses to the loss of a spouse found that women were most vulnerable, in terms of distress, depressive symptomatology, physical symptoms, illness, and mortality immediately after the loss, while men were most vulnerable later. Among elderly persons, Bierhals et al. (1996) found that although widowers exhibited lower mean levels of complicated grief symptomatology than widows in the first two years after they lost their spouse, they experienced higher mean levels in the third, fourth, and fifth years. At the third year measurement, the men's mean levels of complicated grief doubled from their earlier values, while the women's approximately halved.

In non-death losses, grief is not usually measured, but stress is. While stress is not necessarily a marker of mourning, the emergence of stress symptoms (Chiriboga, 1989; Weiss, 1975) -- whether cognitive (e.g., concentration problems, confusion, intrusive thoughts), somatic (e.g., restlessness, agitation, headaches, muscular aches, sensitivity to noise), affective (e.g., sadness, anger, guilt, anxiety and fear), or behavioral symptoms (e.g., crying, obsessive activity, social withdrawal) – are much the same as those that accompany the recognition of the irreversibility of the loss, what Barsky (1993) terms the "reality phase," when denying that something is not as it was before is no longer possible (Barsky, 1993; Martin and Doka, 2000; Oliver, 1999; Schatz, 1986).

Studies of non-death losses show similar gender differences in timing as those found in the studies of responses to death. Thus, in their study of English speaking immigrants to Israel, Walsh and Horenczyk (2001) found that women responded with high levels of stress even before their immigration, while men did not even consider the losses entailed in immigration until after they actually arrived. Empirical studies comparing men's and women's stress and adjustment in divorce found that women experience their highest levels of stress in the period before the decision to divorce is made and prior to the separation, while men experience their highest levels of stress after the decision (Albrecht, 1980; Bloom and Caldwell, 1981; Chiriboga and Cutler, 1977; Harvey, Wells and Alvarez, 1978; Hagestad and Smyer, 1982; Jacobson, 1977). A similar pattern emerges from Riessman and Gerstel's (1985) findings showing that while women tend to be most at risk for developing non-fatal illnesses after separating from their husbands, men tend to be most at risk after the divorce itself. Along similar lines, Diedrich's (1991) review of the empirical literature on divorce adjustment led her to conclude that males reported having experienced less stress than women during the decision and separation period but showed poorer adjustment than women several years after the divorce.

The suggestion that women reach the "reality" phase earlier than men does not mean that all men (or all women) have the same timing in mourning the loss of their marriage. Other factors may be involved: It is likely that men who initiate the separation will begin mourning earlier on in the process, and possibly before the separation itself. In addition, based on his clinical experience, Myers (1989) points out that while some recently separated men engage in massive denial of their loss, other men have mourned completely and most are somewhere in between.

A wife's miscarriage is the only exception found to this pattern thus far. Here, both men and women have been found to respond immediately with strong sadness, depression, anxiety, fear of future losses, guilt, somatic complaints, but men's feelings had abated by half a year post-miscarriage, while women's continued in full strength even two years later.

How

Findings also suggest that men mourn differently from women.

Following death losses, men tend to deny their grief or keep it to themselves and to manifest it indirectly, while women tend to cry, share their feelings and feel depressed. Following the death of a child, Frantz (1984) found that many fathers avoided expressing their feelings. Bohannon (1990) found that husbands scored higher than wives on denial and higher on vigor and physical strength, but lower on despair, guilt, loss of control, rumination, depersonalization, somatization, and death anxiety. Findings on responses to miscarriage show that men report increased blood pressure, physical paining, loss of appetite and exhaustion (Hughes and Page-Lieberman, 1989). In their study of responses to miscarriage and stillbirth, McGreal, Evans and Burrows (1997) found that men were more prone to try to ignore the loss and to avoid talking about it than women and less prone to worry about the matter, to employ coping strategies, including tension reduction, wishful thinking; and seeking spiritual support or a sense of belonging.

Following the death of a spouse, Baarsen and Groenou (2001) found that widowers were less prone than widows to share their emotions with others and to express less expectation of contact and support. At the same time, Stroebe and Stroebe (1983) found that men were more prone to adverse responses, such as depression, physical ailments, death and suicide, than women. With respect to the loss of a parent, Moss, Resch and Moss (1997) found that daughters expressed more emotional upset, somatic response, and continuing tie with the deceased parent than sons, while sons reported more acceptance of the death and greater personal mastery, along with more guilt in relation to being with and caring for their parent. The researchers suggest that this pattern reflects the male style of coping with bereavement, which tends to be more stoic and less expressive, with more emphasis on privacy and less on relationships with and dependency on others.

The pattern of gender differences in the ways of mourning is similar following non-death losses with one addition: intense, sometimes frenetic activity on the part of the man. The literature on divorce indicates that most divorced men respond to their loss by increased activity, somatization, and/or self-medication with alcohol and drugs (e.g., Mandell, 1995;

Umberson and Williams, 1993). McKenry and Price (1991) observe that men are much more likely to quickly replace the marital partner with other sexual partners and to engage in frantic social activity. Riessman (1990) reports that men are much more inclined than women to throw themselves into their work after divorce, to focus the pressure of the loss in the body instead of the emotional life, and, in many cases, to deal with their distress by heavy drinking. In contrast, they are less prone than women to show their grief in depression (Bruce and Kim, 1992; Riessman, 1990), emotional and verbal expression (Riessman, 1990), and seeking emotional help from parents and siblings (Duran-Aydintug, 1998). Where they did want care and nurturance from their parents without having to discuss their distress, they did so indirectly, through appetite loss (Weiner, 1990).

Studies of immigration highlight men's tendency to withdraw or throw themselves into activity, and women's tendency to seek connection. In a study of Israeli high school students who had immigrated from the former USSR, Izikovich (2000) found that most of the boys chose seclusion and isolation, while the girls tried to approach the local youth. In their study of English speaking immigrants to Israel, Walsh and Horenczyk (2001) found that most of the women tried to deal with their losses through connecting with others and seeking emotional support: either through a social support network that became a substitute for the family they had left behind or, in particularly difficult moments, with family in the Russia, whom they telephoned. Men, in contrast, made sure to keep themselves active and busy so as not to feel their losses. They organized trips, hikes, and meals with other immigrants, which enabled them both to meet people and to regain their sense of competence and success.

What

The question of what persons grieve does not arise with respect to death losses, probably because "the deceased" is the first and most obvious answer. Thus, even though it seems possible that the significance of the loss might be different for men and women and that the two might mourn different things in the loss, we have no information on this matter.

With respect to non-death losses, there seem to be different patterns of gender differences in divorce and immigration. Studies of divorce suggest that divorced fathers tend to mourn the loss of their ex-wives considerably less than they mourn the loss of their children and of their home, family life and routine. Jacobs (1983), based on his clinical experience with divorced fathers, states that some men never mourn the loss of their spouse, but concentrate exclusively on mourning changes in their relationship with their children. Riessman (1990), based on interview data of divorced men and women, reports that men tend to mourn the absence of their children and family, rather than the loss of their spouse, while women are more prone to mourn the loss of the marital relationship. Gray and Merrick (1996) present clinical evidence to this effect. Myers (1989) indicates that some men go so far as to deny missing persons they lost in the divorce, whether their children or their wife, but talk about missing things that are symbolic of family, such as their workshop, coming home to an evening meal, or pulling into the driveway and feeling proud of owning a beautiful home.

Studies of immigrants suggest that men tend to mourn losses related to work, while women tend to mourn losses of people and place. In a study of the psychological distress of Soviet immigrants in Israel, Baider, Ever-Hadani and Kaplan DeNour (1996) report that the main source of distress for the men was their loss of earning power, while the main source of distress for the women was their loss of social ties and place. Among English speaking immigrants to Israel, Walsh and Horenczyk (2001) found that while the women tended to mourn the loss of their homes and close relatives, the men tended to mourn the loss of their professional and socio-economic status and their sense of competence and success. While the women tended to concentrate on the things they left behind, the men tend to concentrate on the question weather they will succeed in the new place.

Similar gender differences are found in what other immigrant groups mourn. Hurh and Kim (1990) found that the psychological position of male Korean immigrants in the United States was closely associated with a variety of work related variables, while that of the female immigrants was associated to the well-being of the family and with their ethnic attachments. Jones-Correa (1998) found that male Latino-American immigrants to New-York City experienced a sharp decrease in their professional status.

In short, findings consistently show that men mourn both death and non-death losses differently from women: They often begin their morning later. They tend to less direct emotional expression, whether alone or with others, and greater denial or stoicism, but also to more indirect forms of expression, including both hyper-activity and self-medication with alcohol. Exactly what they mourn when they divorce or immigrate is also different. These differences mean that clinicians cannot properly proceed as they would with women clients and, for optimal results, must take men's particular ways of mourning into consideration. The remainder of this chapter offers practical suggestions for how to tailor their counseling to men's distinct needs.

When and How to Offer Help

The fact that men seek little help in general and in coping with non-death losses in particular means that help must be offered to them. That is, there must be reaching out to men by professionals in public and voluntary agencies. The reaching out should be done bearing in mind the importance of proper timing and the perceptions and feelings that may deter men from seeking help.

Timing the outreach properly means offering help when the opportunity is available and when the man will be most likely to accept the help or, conversely, least likely to reject it. Since men initially respond to most losses with denial, anger, withdrawal, or hyper-activity, and generally begin to feel their sadness and grief only as the months go by, offers of help should be made not only immediately upon the loss, but in the months and, sometimes, years afterwards as well. Attending to the perceptions and feelings that deter men from seeking help means offering help in manner that circumvents the association men may make between help seeking and weakness or ineptness, and, where suitable, enhances the man's self-perception of doing right by his family. It also means offering the help in incremental steps so as to enable the man to retain a sense of control. While persons' need for control varies with their personality, control generally tends to be important for men (Bay and Braver, 1990). To maximize the man's control, initial contact might be better by telephone than in person. A meeting might be suggested without requiring an immediate response, and the therapist would ask if it's all right to phone again at a later date. Where the man hesitates or refuses, he might be offered a trial meeting, at any point in the future, with no obligation to continue.

The application of these principles would vary from one type of loss to another. It is perhaps simplest in cases of loss through death, as such losses are visible and clear, and men's mourning them is relatively well legitimized. As indicated in the extensive literature written on helping men with bereavement (e.g., Gray, 2001; Martin and Doka, 2000), offers of help can be made fairly soon after the death and as a direct offer of help in dealing with the bereavement.

The application is more complicated in non-death losses, since the very existence of the loss is not always recognized. In cases of miscarriage, the hospital setting provides the first opportunity to offer help. Help can be offered to both spouses when the woman is first released from the hospital after the miscarriage (Gray, 2001). Then, when the woman comes for a follow-up, whether to the hospital or ambulatory clinic, the doctor or nurse can relate briefly to what both spouses are feeling. This type of intervention is not therapy, but relays to both spouses the legitimacy of the man's grief following a miscarriage. As for actual therapy, this should be offered to either or both spouses. In situations where the man will not accept help on his own, the professional would treat both spouses' coping with the loss.

Following divorce, efforts should be made to time the offer of help to the stage in the divorce process when men begin to sense what they have lost with the breakup of their marriage. Prior to that, there tends to be a period of denial, when men who initiate the divorce tend to feel primarily relief at ending an unsatisfactory relationship, and men who do not want the divorce may still hope that they can avert it. Neither is likely to seek help.

Given that different men become aware of their losses in divorce at different times, the timing of the offer of help can only be approximate. Nonetheless, since, as noted above, men begin to sense their losses in divorce relatively late in the process, generally only after the actual separation (Baum, 2003), offers of emotional help should probably be directed to men who have already separated from their wives, rather than those who have not, and be repeated for some time after the legal divorce.

With respect to how, the help might be offered to "divorced fathers" rather than to "divorced men". This framing would allow divorced fathers to seek help without feeling they are doing so only for themselves or because they cannot cope and would make their help seeking a positive, ego-enhancing act on behalf of themselves and their children both. It may also bolster their ability to expose their grief and to experience the pain, sadness, and other unpleasant and "unmasculine" emotions that are likely to arise in the course of their treatment.

Immigrants would best be offered help after they have settled into the new country for a while and have tacked the immediate practical problems entailed in the process. Offers of help might be made in connecting with the tasks the man faces in his new country, such as finding work, fathering in the new culture, and building a new social life. Where the man is uninclined to accept help on his own or even with his wife and children, attempts might be made to reach him when offering help to the wife and children.

THE THERAPEUTIC PROCESS

The major task in non-death losses therapy is to help the individual to mourn the losses inherent in the event, whether divorce, miscarriage, immigration, or other. This is important not only because of the intrinsic difficulties of the mourning process, but also because, in contrast to mourning loss through bereavement, there are no recognized rites or rituals to mourn these losses. In addition, for men there is little social recognition of the grief resulting from divorce, miscarriage or immigration and little societal support for the working-through process.

The clinician must thus provide the recognition and support that are not provided by the society. Most men who seek therapy following divorce, miscarriage or immigration ask for help with practical problems or problems in functioning. After divorce it might be sexual problems, problems in forming a new relationship, problems in parenting and, in a relatively few cases, somatic problems. After miscarriage it might be sexual problems, marital problems, or problems at work. After immigration men may ask for help finding work and adjusting to the new work environment, marital strains, and problems with their children. Few men come saying that they want help in mourning their losses or even in dealing with the confusion of emotions that is generally attend such losses. Many men, even after the denial phase, will tell that, aside from the presenting problem, everything is just fine.

The clinician's first job is to help their male clients to recognize their losses and to acknowledge them as losses. It is generally better not to use the word 'loss,' which the man might find alien or deny. Instead, it is preferable to ask what the men miss from the life they had before the divorce/miscarriage/immigration. In cases of miscarriage, the questions might focus on the expectations the man had and no longer has after the loss of the unborn child. After divorce, relatively few men will readily talk about the good things in their lives or tell what they miss. Clinicians should not be surprised by assertions that nothing was good and there is nothing to miss or by their clients' need to dwell on the problems and unhappiness that led to their divorce and to allocate blame. Clinicians should not be deterred, however, from gently pressing the issue and returning to it after room has been made for the men to work through their negative feelings, when they feel more comfortable in the therapeutic relationship, and when they are better able to confront their losses.

Clinicians should not be surprised if their male clients are initially able to speak of their losses only indirectly. Following miscarriage, some men will feel more comfortable speaking of their wife's loss and grief than of their own. Following immigration, some men will prefer speaking of their wife's and children's longing for the old country than of their own. Clinicians should be aware that in such cases, talking about the losses and grief of others is the only means, albeit indirect, that the man has of expressing his own loss and grief, and allow them to do so.

Following divorce, most men find it considerably easier to speak of the loss of their pre-divorce family life and relationship with their children than the loss of their wives. It is important that clinicians realize that the absence of overt expression does not necessarily mean an absence of grief for the loss of the ex-wife. What it does mean is that before helping their male clients to work through the loss of their ex-wife, they must first help their clients to work through the losses that are more obvious to them.

For mourning to occur, the cognitive identification of the losses must become an emotional realization, with the man experiencing the sadness and pain attendant on his losses. In most cases, this experience will be blocked by a wall of anger. Anger is a dominant emotion in the wake of loss, among men and women both. It tends to be more accessible to men, however. It is a socially acceptable response among men (Erickson, 1993) and thus may be easier for men to express and cope with than grief and sorrow, and also serve as a defense against these emotions (Candib, 1995). Therapists should not be misled by the expressions of anger, sometimes very intense, usually supported with a plethora of concrete grievances, into thinking that the man does not feel grief.

Before helping the male client to work through the underlying grief, the therapist must let him know that it is alright to feel and express anger. With this, though, the therapist should lead the men to connect with the underlying sorrow and loss. For many men, this connection can come only after the therapist confirms that they have cause for grief and lets them know that it is alright to grieve – that grieving is not unmanly. Statements such as "When people lose things, it arouses a lot of feelings" and "Some people think that grieving is weak and unmanly" may be helpful. Simply verbalizing the possibility of an emotional response gives permission for it, and may leave room for patients to later acknowledge their grief.

With assistance from the therapist, some men will be able to acknowledge and express their grief openly. Therapists can help such men by putting into words the inchoate feelings that they may have but cannot sort out or articulate (Freund, 1974; Myers, 1989). For men who are wary of expressing their sadness, the therapist may help by asking them to describe their grief without using the word feeling, for example by asking, "How is it for you?" Men who respond to such questions with an account or demonstration of their sadness benefit from the prompting, and may need it. Other men, as writers on bereavement note, will be able to cry or break down only when they are alone (Staudacher, 1991). Such men may prefer to mourn their losses in private, and therapists should respect this preference.

The goal need not be to get men to express their grief in words, tears, or in some other direct way. As Carverhill (1997) points out in connection with bereavement, the expectation that they do so is based on a female model of mourning. Instead, therapists should recognize that, as noted above, many divorced men act out their grief, and should understand their frenetic hyperactivity, self-medication, and somatization, where these occur, as indirect expressions of grief and sorrow. The therapist's task is to help men who act out their grief to connect their behaviors with their underlying feelings.

The above points refer mainly to individual intervention. In situations where both spouses come to treatment, one of the key aims is to help both of them to recognize not only their own grief, but also that of their spouse. Information about differences in the ways that men and women mourn can help to legitimize the man's way of mourning and will allow each spouse to understand and respect the grief of the other, to give up the expectation that the spouse will mourn exactly as he/she does, and allow each the space to mourn in their own way. This, in turn, will increase the couple's sense of sharing and togetherness.

TERMINATION OF TREATMENT

As has been repeatedly noted, treatment termination is both a difficult and a highly significant phase of the therapeutic process, which may impact on the ability of the patient to maintain the changes attained in the course of the therapy (Anthony and Pagano, 1998; Baum, 2005; Fortune, 1987; Fortune, Pearlingi and Rochelle,1992; Kramer, 1990; Marx and Gelso, 1987). It is a particularly critical and sensitive phase of grief therapy, because, like the death, divorce, immigration or miscarriage itself, the end of treatment involves the loss of an important relationship. The separation from the therapist may thus re-activate the feelings inherent in these events. Moreover, the work on loss that figured as the key theme of the therapy will have sensitized the patient to the loss inherent in treatment termination (Baum, 2005; Boyer and Hoffman, 1993).

Attaining proper closure is thus particularly important in grief therapy. Where the patient decides to cease treatment on his own, the therapist should make every effort to persuade him to return for at least one more session, possibly several, to express his feelings and thoughts about the therapy. Though not every patient will be amenable to persuasion, the therapist should, as far as possible, try to prevent too abrupt a bolting. When the decision to terminate is the therapist's, whether alone or shared with the patient, care should be taken to leave enough time for the feelings that arise at termination, and especially feelings associated with loss, to emerge and for the patient to be able to express them. Clinicians would do well to take into account that some of their male patients may return to former patterns of denial and that they need encouragement to express their feelings about the impending separation. Clinicians should also take into account the possibility that issues that were thought to have been resolved will suddenly re-arise with the termination and should offer the patient the opportunity to work on them.

REFERENCES

Abboud, L. N., and Liamputtong, P. (2003). Pregnancy loss: What it means to women who miscarry and their partners. *Social Work in Health Care, 36*, 37-62.

Albrecht, S. (1980). Reactions and adjustment to divorce: Differences in the experiences of males and females. *Family Relations, 29*, 59-68.

Anthony, S., and Pagano, G. (1998). The therapeutic potential for growth during the termination process. *Clinical Social Work Journal, 26* (3), 281-295.

Arendell, T. (1992). The social self as gendered: A masculinist discourse of divorce. *Symbolic Interaction, 15* (2), 151-181.

Baarsen, B., and Groenou, M. (2001). Partner loss in latter life: Gender differences in coping shortly after bereavement. *Journal of Loss and Trauma, 6*, 243-262.

Baider, L., Ever-Hadani, P., and Kaplan DeNour, A. (1996). Crossing new bridges: The process of adaptation and psychological distress of Russian immigrants in Israel. *Psychiatry, 59*(2), 175-183.

Barsky, M. (1993). When grief underlies the conflict. *Mediation Quarterly, 11* (1), 39-53.

Baum, N. (2003). The male way of mourning divorce: When, what and how. *Clinical Social Work Journal, 31* (1), 37-50.

Baum, N. (2005). Correlates of clients' emotional and behavioral responses to treatment termination. *Clinical Social Work Journal, 33*(3), 309-326.

Bay, R., and Braver, S. (1990). Perceived control of the divorce settlement process and interparental conflict. *Family Relations, 39*, 382-387.

Bierhals, A., Frank, E., Prigerson, H., Miller, M., Fasiczka, A., and Reynolds, C. (1996). Gender differences in complicated grief among the elderly. *Omega: Journal of Death and Dying, 32*, 303-317.

Bloom, B., and Caldwell, R. (1981). Sex differences in adjustment during the process of marital separation. *Journal of Marriage and the Family, 43*, 693-701.

Bohannon, R. (1990). Grief responses of spouses following the death of a child: A longitudinal study. *Omega: Journal of Death and Dying, 22* (2), 109–121

Boyer, P., and Hoffman, A. (1993). Counselor affective reactions to termination: Impact of counselor loss history and perceived client sensitivity to loss. *Journal of Counseling Psychology, 40*, 271-277.

Bruce, M., and Kim, K. (1992). Differences in the effects of divorce on major depression in men and women. *American Journal of Psychiatry, 149*, 914-917.

Bryant, M. (1989). Commentary: Fathers grieve, too. *Journal of Perinatology, 9*, 437-441.

Candib, L. (1995). *Medicine and the family: A feminist perspective*. New York: Basic Books.

Carroll, R., and Shaefer, S. (1993-1994). Similarities and differences in spouses coping with sides. *Omega, 28*, 273-284.

Carverhill, P. (1997). Bereaved men: How therapists can help. *Psychotherapy in Private Practice, 16* (4), 1-15.

Cecil, R. (1994). "I wouldn't have minded a wee one running about": Miscarriage and the family. *Social Science and Medicine, 38*, 1415-1422.

Chiriboga, D. (1989). Divorce at midlife. In R.A. Kalish (Ed.). *Midlife loss, coping strategies* (pp. 179-217). London: Sage.

Chiriboga, D., and Cutler, L. (1977). Stress responses among divorcing men and women. *Journal of Divorce, 1*, 95-106.

Cook, J. (1988). Dad's double binds. *Journal of Contemporary Ethnography, 17* (3), 285-308.

Corney, R. H. (1990). Sex differences in general practice attendance and help-seeking for minor illness. *Journal of Psychosomatic Research, 34*, 525-534.

Day, R.D., and Hook, D. (1987). Miscarriage: A special type of family crisis. *Family Relations, 36*, 305-310.

De Frain, J., Martens, L., Stork, J., and Stork, W. (1990-91). The psychological effects of a stillbirth on surviving family members. *Omega, 22*, 81-108.

Diedrich, P. (1991). Gender differences in divorce adjustment. In: S. Volgy (Ed.). *Women and divorce men and divorce*. New York: The Haworth Press.

Dion K.K., and Dion, K.L. (2001) Gender and cultural adaptation in immigrant families. *The Journal of Social Issues, 57* (3), 511-521.

Doka, K. J. (1989). Disenfranchised grief. In K. J. Doka (Ed.), *Disenfranchised grief: Recognizing hidden sorrow* (pp. 3-11). Lexington, MA: Lexington Books.

Douglas, J. (1990-91). Patterns of change following parent death in midlife adults. *Omega: Journal of Death and Dying, 22*, 123-137.

Duran-Aydintug, C. (1998). Emotional support during separation: Its sources and determinants, *Journal of Divorce and Remarriage, 29* (3/4), 121-141.

Erickson, B. (1993). *Helping men change the role of the female therapist*. London: Sage Publications.

Fish, W. (1986). Differences of grief intensity in bereaved parents. In. T. Rando (Ed.) *Parental loss of a child* (pp. 415-428). Champaign IL: Research Press.

Fisher, J.D., Nadler, A., and Whitcher-Alagna, S. (1982). Recipients' reactions to aid. *Psychological Bulleting, 91,* 27-54.

Fortune, A. (1987). Grief only? Client and social worker reactions to termination. *Clinical Social Work Journal, 15*(2), 159-171.

Fortune A., Pearlingi, B., and Rochelle, C. (1992). Reaction to termination of individual treatment, *Social Work, 37* (2), 171-178.

Frantz, T. (1984). Helping parents whose child has died. In: T. Frantz (Ed.) *Death and grief in the family* (pp. 11-26). Rockville, MD: Aspen Systems.

Freund J. (1974). Divorce and grief. *Journal of Family Counseling, 2* (2), 40-43.

Gilbert, K (1996). "We've had the same loss, why don't we have the same grief?" Loss and differential grief in families. *Death Studies, 20* (3), 269-283.

Gilbert, K., and Smart, L. S. (1992). *Coping with infant or fetal loss: The couple's healing process*. New York: Brunner-Mazel.

Gray, C., and Merrick, D.S. (1996). Voice alterations, why women have more difficulty than men with the legal process of divorce. *Family and Conciliation Courts Review, 34* (2), 240-251.

Gray, K. (2001). Grieving reproductive loss: The Bereaved male. In D. Lund (Ed.), *Men coping with grief. Death, value and meaning cries* (pp. 327-337). N.Y.: Baywood Publishing Co.

Hagestad, G., and Smyer, M. (1982). Dissolving long-term relationships: Patterns of divorcing in middle age. In S. Duch (Ed.). *Personal relationships*. London: Academic Press.

Harvey, J.H., Wells, G.L., and Alvarez, M.D. (1978). Attribution in the context of conflict and separation in close relationships. In J. H. Harvey, W. Ickes, and R. Kidd (Eds.). *New directives in attribution research*. New Jersey: Lawrence Erlbaum Associates.

Hobfoll, E., and Lerman, M. (1989). Predicting receipt of social support: A longitudinal study of parents' reactions to their child's illness. *Health Psychology, 2,* 82-91.

Hughes, C., and Page-Lieberman, J. (1989). Fathers experiencing a perinatal loss, *Death-Studies, 13* (6), 537-556

Hurh, W., and Kim, K. (1990). Correlates of Korean immigrants' mental health. The *Journal of Nervous and Mental Disease, 178,* 703-711.

Izikovich, R. (2000). Gender differences in cross-cultural adaptation styles of immigrant youths from the former USSR in Israel. *Youth and Society, 31,* 310-331.

Jacobs, J. (1983). Treatment of divorcing fathers: Social and psychotherapeutic considerations. *American Journal of Psychiatry, 140* (10), 1294-1299.

Jacobson, G. (1977). *The multiple crises of marital separation and divorce*. New York: Grune and Stratton.

Jones-Correa, M. (1998). Different Paths: Gender, Immigration and Political Participation. *International Migration Review, 32* (2), 326-349.

Kimble, D. (1991). Neonatal death: A descriptive study of fathers' experience. *Neonatal Network, 9* (8), 45-50.

Kramer, S. (1990). *Positive endings in psychotherapy: Bringing meaningful closure to therapeutic relationships*. San Francisco, CA: Jossey-Bass.

Lehr, R., and MacMillan, P. (2001). The psychological and emotional impact of divorce: The noncustodial fathers' perspective. *Families in Society: The Journal of Contemporary Human Services, 82*(4), 373-382.

Mandell, D. (1995). Fathers who don't pay child support: Hearing their voices. *Journal of Divorce and Remarriage, 23* (1/2), 85-116.

Martin, T., and Doka, K. (2000). *Men don't cry women do*. Philadelphia: Brunner/Mazel.

Marx, J., and Gelso, C. (1987). Termination of individual counseling in a university counseling center. *Journal of Counseling Psychology, 34* (1), 3-9.

McGreal, D., Evans, B. J., and Burrows, G. D. (1997). Gender differences in coping following loss of a child through miscarriage or stillbirth: A pilot study. *Stress Medicine, 13*, 159-165.

McKenry, P., and Price, S. (1991). Alternatives for support: Life after divorce – A literature review. *Journal of Divorce and Remarriage, 15* (3/4), 1-19.

Meth, R., and Pasick, R. (1990). *Men in therapy: The challenge of change*. New York: Guildford Press.

Moss, M., Resch, N., and Moss, S. (1997). The role of gender in middle-age children's responses to parent death. *Omega, 35* (1), 43-65.

Murray, J., Terry, D., Vance, J., Battistutta, D., and Connolly, Y. (2000). Effects of a program of intervention on parental distress following infant death. *Death Studies, 24*, 275-305.

Myers, M. (1989). *Men and divorce*. New York: The Guilford Press.

Neugebauer, R., Kline, J., O'Connor, P., Shrout, P., Johnson, J., Skodol, A., Wicks, J., and Susser, M. (1992). Determinants of depressive symptoms in early weeks after miscarriage. *American Journal of Public Health, 82*, 1332-1339.

Oakley, A., McPherson, A., and Roberts, H. (1990). *Miscarriage*. London: Penguin.

Oliver, L. (1999). Effects of a child's death on the marital relationship: A review. *Omega: Journal of Death and Dying, 39*, 197-227.

Puddifoot, J. E., and Johnson, M. P. (1997). The legitimacy of grieving: The partner's experience at miscarriage. *Social Science and Medicine, 45*: 837-845.

Puddifoot, J. E., and Johnson, M. P. (1999). Active grief, despair, and difficulty coping: Some measured characteristics of male response following their partner's miscarriage. *Journal of Reproductive and Infant Psychology, 17*, 89-93.

Rickwood, D. J., and Braithwaite, V. A. (1994). Social psychological factors affecting help-seeking for emotional problems. *Social Science and Medicine, 39*, 563-572.

Riessman, C. (1990). *Divorce talk: Women and men make sense of personal relationships*. New Brunswick: Rudgers University Press.

Riessman, C., and Gerstel, N. (1985). Marital dissolution and health: Do males or females have greater risk? *Social Science Mediation, 20* (6), 627-635.

Salgado de Snyder, N., Cervantes, R., and Padilla, A. (1990). Gender and ethnic differences in psychosocial stress and generalized distress among Hispanics. *Sex Roles, 22* (7/8), 441-453.

Schatz, W. (1986). Grief of fathers. In T. Rando (Ed.). *Parental loss of a child* (pp. 293-302). Champaign, IL: Research Press Company.

Shapiro, A., and Lambert, J. (1999). Longitudinal effects of divorce on the quality of the father-child relationship and on fathers' psychological well-being. *Journal of Marriage and the Family, 61*, 397-408.

Staudacher, C. (1991). *Men and Grief.* Oakland, California: New Harbinger.

Stinson, K. M., Lasker, J. N., Lohmann, J., and Toedter, L. J. (1992). Parents grief following pregnancy loss: a comparison of mothers and fathers. *Family Relations, 41*, 218-223.

Stroebe, M., and Stroebe, W. (1983). Who suffers more? Sex differences in health risks of the widowed. *Psychological Bulletin, 93* (2), 279-301.

Stroebe, M., Stroebe, W., and Schut, H. (2001). Gender differences in adjustment to bereavement: An empirical and theoretical review. *Review of General Psychology, 5*(1), 62-83.

Umberson, D., and Williams, C. (1993). Divorced fathers, parental role strain and psychological distress. *Journal of Family Issues, 14* (3), 378-400.

Walsh, S., and Horenczyk, V. (2001). Gendered patterns of experience in social and cultural transition: The case of English-speaking immigrants in Israel. *Sex Roles, 45* (7/8), 501-528.

Weiner, E. (1990). *Bowen's concept of emotional connectedness to former spouse and family of origin as a moderator of health in a divorced population: A partial test of Bowen theory.* Unpublished doctoral dissertation, Kansas State University.

Weiss, S. (1975). *Marital separation.* New York: Basic Books.

INDEX

A

academic performance, 87, 88
academic success, 88
access, ix, 12, 47, 63, 64
accountability, 89
accounting, 11
acculturation, 33
achievement, x, 83, 87, 88
adaptability, 54
adaptation, 28, 43, 105, 106, 107
adjustment, x, 28, 29, 36, 42, 43, 83, 87, 95, 98, 105, 106, 109
administration, 51, 52, 57
administrators, x, 83, 85, 88
adolescence, 73, 87
adolescents, vii, 4, 16, 19, 21, 81, 90, 92
adults, vii, 9, 16, 21, 73, 75, 76, 80, 88, 106
advertisements, 6
advertising, 7
affective reactions, 106
African American, 31, 32, 33, 34, 38, 57, 62, 83, 84, 87, 92
African American women, 33
African Americans, 32, 92
afternoon, 35
age, viii, 6, 11, 23, 25, 28, 29, 30, 36, 44, 62, 72, 73, 79, 87, 107, 108
aggression, 2, 4, 13, 14, 15, 19
aggressive behavior, viii, 1, 18, 87
AIDS, 57
alcohol, 36, 99, 101
alternative(s), 49, 52, 53, 85
ambivalence, 44
American Psychiatric Association, 80
American Psychological Association, 43, 85, 86, 90, 91, 93, 94
anger, 2, 87, 92, 97, 98, 101, 104

anger management, 87
anti-cancer, 44
anxiety, vii, 2, 28, 60, 98, 99
appetite, 100
arousal, 2
assessment, 28, 31, 33, 35, 66, 93
assignment, 63, 66, 67
asthma, 51, 57
asymptomatic, 19
attachment, 73
attention, vii, 1, 52, 76, 77, 80, 95, 96
attitudes, viii, 1, 10, 19, 21, 70
attribution, 107
Australia, 97
authority, 16
autism, ix, 71, 72, 73, 74, 75, 76, 77, 78, 79, 80, 81, 82
availability, 52
avoidance, 78
awareness, 4, 7, 10, 21, 58

B

barriers, ix, 10, 11, 12, 13, 14, 15, 17, 32, 47, 91
BD, 58
behavior, x, 3, 4, 9, 10, 11, 12, 13, 15, 16, 17, 18, 19, 22, 26, 37, 41, 63, 64, 65, 71, 72, 73, 74, 76, 77, 78, 79, 80, 81, 87, 88, 92
behavioral disorders, 90, 93
behavioral problems, 76, 86
beliefs, 5, 10, 13, 14, 15, 18, 21, 73
beneficial effect, 3, 39
benefits, ix, x, 3, 10, 11, 13, 14, 15, 17, 32, 41, 47, 51, 52, 55, 56, 72, 79, 83, 88
blame, 2, 103
blood, 99
blood pressure, 99
body image, 27, 28
bonding, 28, 41

boys, 72, 87, 92, 100
Breast, 23, 24, 25, 34, 43, 44, 45, 56
breast cancer, viii, 23, 25, 26, 27, 28, 29, 30, 31, 32, 33, 34, 36, 40, 41, 42, 43, 44, 45, 56, 58
breast self-examination, 10
bullying, 85

C

California, 23, 29, 35, 109
Canada, 97
cancer, viii, 23, 24, 25, 26, 27, 28, 30, 31, 32, 34, 36, 39, 40, 42, 43, 44, 45, 56
cancer screening, 25
cancer treatment, 26, 28, 30, 31, 39
cardiac surgery, 49, 57
cell, 40
CFI, 13
chemotherapy, 25, 30, 33, 40, 56
childcare, 35
childhood, 73, 89, 90
childhood disorders, 89
children, vii, x, 25, 29, 36, 71, 72, 73, 75, 76, 77, 78, 79, 80, 81, 83, 84, 85, 86, 87, 88, 89, 90, 91, 92, 93, 94, 96, 98, 100, 102, 103, 108
Chinese, 31, 32, 34
Chinese women, 32
chronic diseases, 51
Cincinnati, 71, 83
classes, 61, 68
classroom, 27, 60, 61, 66, 75, 77, 79, 87, 88
classroom management, 88
classrooms, 77
clients, ix, 57, 59, 60, 61, 62, 63, 64, 66, 67, 68, 101, 103, 106
clinical psychology, vii, viii, 1, 5
clinical trials, 26
close relationships, 20, 107
closure, 105, 108
coding, 32
coercion, 20
cognitive function, 79
cognitive impairment, 79, 82
cognitive process, 49, 63, 92
cohort, 28
collaboration, 87
college students, 5, 36
colon, 56
colon cancer, 56
colonoscopy, 49, 57
communication, viii, 3, 15, 17, 21, 23, 30, 36, 37, 48, 50, 53, 61, 72, 73, 76, 80, 81
communication skills, 76, 80
community, x, 5, 9, 12, 16, 26, 34, 35, 36, 48, 55, 83, 84, 85, 86, 89, 91, 93, 97
community service, 55
compatibility, 20
competence, 69, 70, 93, 100, 101
competency, 48, 97
complement, 63
complications, 48
components, x, 83
composition, 27, 29, 30, 67
comprehension, 54, 77
computed tomography, 51, 52
computers, 54
concentration, 98
conceptualization, 4, 69
concrete, 104
conduct problems, 87
confidence, 64, 65
confidentiality, 63
conflict, 3, 4, 21, 105, 107
conflict resolution, 4
confrontation, 26
confusion, 74, 98, 103
Congress, iv
consciousness, 41
consensus, 25
consent, 52, 55, 57, 85
construction, 13
constructive communication, 4
constructivist learning, 56
consultants, 33
consumers, 91
control, 3, 4, 11, 26, 27, 28, 35, 36, 37, 40, 44, 51, 68, 74, 75, 79, 87, 98, 99, 101, 106
control condition, 26, 37
control group, 3, 4, 28, 35, 40, 68
controlled trials, 21
coping strategies, 99, 106
coronary artery disease, 51
correlation, 15
correlations, 14
cost effectiveness, 53
costs, 54
counsel, 66
counseling, vii, viii, ix, 2, 3, 5, 6, 7, 8, 9, 11, 12, 17, 21, 22, 24, 35, 36, 37, 39, 41, 42, 51, 57, 59, 60, 61, 62, 63, 64, 65, 66, 67, 68, 69, 70, 101, 108
counseling psychology, vii
couples, vii, viii, 1, 2, 3, 5, 6, 7, 8, 9, 10, 11, 12, 16, 17, 19, 20, 22, 97
credentials, 8
credit, 62
criticism, 3

crying, 76, 95, 98
cues, 74, 77, 81
cultural differences, 32
cultural transition, 109
culture, 28, 102
curriculum, 4, 85

D

data analysis, 69
data base, 42
data collection, 75
dating, 3, 4, 12, 13, 14, 16, 17, 18, 19, 20, 21, 22
death, x, 95, 96, 97, 98, 99, 100, 101, 102, 103, 105, 106, 107, 108
decision making, 51
decisions, x, 29, 41, 54, 71
defense, 104
definition, 51
delivery, ix, 47, 48, 53, 55
demographic characteristics, 29, 30
demographic factors, 36
demographics, 19
denial, ix, 24, 41, 98, 99, 101, 102, 103, 105
depersonalization, 98, 99
depression, vii, 26, 28, 31, 36, 42, 44, 95, 99, 100
depressive symptomatology, 98
depressive symptoms, 108
desire, ix, 9, 32, 47, 55, 67, 72, 80
desires, 73
developmental delay, 73, 81
developmental disorder, 80
diabetes, 51
Diagnostic and Statistical Manual of Mental Disorders, 72
Difference of a Difference model, viii, 23
directives, 107
disability, 28, 30
disclosure, 7, 32
discourse, 105
disease activity, 51
disorder, 71, 72, 80, 81
distress, vii, viii, 1, 2, 3, 5, 6, 7, 8, 10, 12, 16, 17, 18, 21, 26, 27, 28, 29, 30, 36, 37, 39, 42, 97, 98, 100, 101, 108
distribution, 33
diversity, 67
divorce, x, 3, 7, 8, 9, 10, 11, 12, 16, 21, 95, 96, 98, 99, 100, 101, 102, 103, 105, 106, 107, 108, 109
divorce rates, 3, 10
doctors, 12
domestic violence, 21
Down syndrome, 81

downward comparison, viii, 24, 40
drug use, 57
drugs, 36, 99
DSM, 72, 80
DSM-IV, 72, 80
durability, 4
duration, 61, 77, 78
duties, 50
DVD, 54
dysphoria, viii, 24, 26, 30, 31, 38

E

earning power, 101
eating, 36, 76, 78
echolalia, 76
economic status, 101
education, ix, 3, 7, 8, 19, 20, 21, 22, 25, 26, 27, 28, 30, 32, 33, 36, 38, 40, 42, 43, 44, 47, 48, 49, 50, 51, 53, 54, 55, 56, 57, 59, 62, 69, 81, 88, 89, 90, 93
educational process, 87, 88
educational programs, 56
educators, 21, 59, 60
ego, 102
Einstein, 47
elderly, ix, 44, 47, 53, 98, 106
elementary school, 75, 87, 90, 93
email, 71
emergency physician, 50
emotion, 104
emotional distress, 26, 98
emotional well-being, 39
emotions, 31, 60, 73, 87, 99, 102, 103, 104
empathy, 60, 63, 68, 69, 73
empowerment, x, 83, 91
encouragement, 26, 64, 65, 105
energy, 30
engagement, 77, 80
England, 97
enthusiasm, 37
environment, 8, 49, 74, 88
episiotomy, 56
equipment, 62
equity, 4
ethics, 69
ethnic background, 32
ethnic diversity, 35
ethnic groups, 2, 25, 84
ethnic minority, 84
ethnicity, viii, 24, 28, 36, 37, 39, 41, 43, 62
etiquette, 78
Euro, 29, 31, 32, 34

evening, 31, 35, 100
evidence, vii, viii, 1, 3, 5, 6, 22, 23, 24, 25, 86, 88, 89, 91, 94, 100
evidence-based practices, 89
exercise, 27, 28, 64
experimental condition, viii, 23
experimental design, viii, 23, 35
expertise, 8, 54, 85
exposure, 9, 32
external locus of control, 28

F

facial expression, 72
facilitators, 34, 35, 42
factor analysis, 11, 13
failure, 72, 73, 92
family, 7, 8, 9, 19, 26, 29, 30, 32, 42, 53, 61, 62, 86, 88, 95, 96, 100, 101, 103, 106, 107, 109
family environment, 8
family interactions, 9
family life, 100, 103
family members, 26, 53, 86, 88, 106
family relationships, 29
family support, 32
family therapy, 86
fat, 36
fatigue, 30, 31
fear, 32, 74, 98, 99
feedback, 9, 35, 60, 63, 64, 66, 67, 68, 78, 81
feelings, 26, 27, 32, 63, 64, 65, 95, 96, 97, 99, 101, 103, 104, 105
feet, 19
females, 4, 8, 73, 78, 105, 108
fidelity, 84, 89, 90, 91, 92
Filipino, 31
five-factor model, 13
focus groups, viii, 6, 10, 21, 23, 28, 29, 31, 32, 33, 41, 42, 44
focusing, 2, 15, 75, 85
food, 78
formal education, 27
framing, 102
funding, x, 83, 89

G

gender, 4, 7, 8, 14, 43, 98, 99, 100, 101, 108
gender differences, 98, 99, 100, 101
gender stereotyping, 4
generalization, 79
generation, 19

genetic counselling, 56
Geneva, 93
genre, 55
geography, 33
Georgia, 72
Gestalt, 62
girls, 72, 78, 100
goals, 4, 26, 49, 75
graduate students, ix, 59, 62, 63
grief, 96, 97, 98, 99, 100, 101, 102, 103, 104, 105, 106, 107, 108, 109
group activities, 78
group interactions, 76
group therapy, 26, 44, 45, 87
groups, viii, ix, 4, 6, 8, 9, 11, 15, 23, 24, 26, 27, 29, 31, 32, 33, 34, 35, 40, 41, 42, 43, 44, 84, 92, 97, 101
growth, x, 41, 83, 89, 105
guidance, 79
guidelines, 27, 74, 75, 84
guilt, 98, 99

H

hair loss, 30
hands, 66, 76
harassment, 85
harm, 8, 16, 75, 92
harmony, 8
Hawaii, 85, 90, 93
Health Belief Model (HBM), viii, 2, 10, 11, 12, 13, 14, 17, 18
HD, 86, 94
healing, 107
health, vii, viii, ix, x, 1, 10, 13, 19, 20, 21, 22, 27, 28, 29, 30, 31, 36, 37, 47, 48, 49, 50, 51, 53, 55, 58, 83, 84, 85, 88, 89, 90, 92, 93, 97, 108, 109
health care, ix, 47, 48, 49, 50, 51
health care system, 48, 49, 51
health education, ix, 47, 48, 50, 51, 55
health information, ix, 47, 48, 50, 53
health insurance, 29
health problems, 19, 28
health services, x, 21, 83, 88, 89, 90
health status, 29, 30, 36
heavy drinking, 100
high school, 20, 29, 100
hip, 41
Hispanic, 34, 38, 62
Hispanics, 108
HIV, 49, 51, 52, 55, 57, 58
HIV test, 49, 51, 53, 55
homework, 76

hospitals, 35, 57, 58, 97
hotels, 35
human behavior, 17
hyperactivity, 104
hypnosis, 26

I

identification, 104
idiosyncratic, 18, 72
illiteracy, 57
imagination, 73
immigrants, 57, 97, 98, 100, 101, 105, 107, 109
immigration, x, 48, 95, 96, 98, 100, 103, 105
immune function, 2
impairments, 72
implementation, x, 50, 68, 74, 78, 83, 84, 85, 89, 90, 91, 93
incidence, 2, 25
inclusion, 7
income, ix, x, 6, 11, 14, 47, 58, 83, 84, 87, 92
indication, 9
indicators, 88
indices, 20
inequality, 4
infancy, 55, 73
informed consent, 51, 52, 53, 56, 57, 58, 62
inhibition, 96
injury, iv
insight, 7, 8
instruction, 26, 45, 56, 66, 88
instructional methods, 7
instructors, 61
instruments, 29
insurance, 48
integration, vii
integrity, 86, 91, 93
intelligence, 79
intensity, 37, 72, 107
intentions, viii, ix, 2, 13, 14, 15, 71, 73
interaction, ix, 20, 21, 39, 71, 72, 73, 76, 79
Interaction, 57, 105
interactional perspective, 19
interactions, viii, 24, 37, 40, 49, 73, 74, 75, 76, 78, 87
internal validity, 65, 90
internalizing, 49
internship, 68
interparental conflict, 106
interpersonal relations, 5, 41
interpersonal relationships, 5
interpretation, 65

intervention, vii, viii, ix, 1, 2, 3, 23, 24, 25, 26, 27, 28, 29, 32, 33, 34, 35, 36, 37, 38, 39, 40, 41, 42, 44, 48, 49, 57, 71, 74, 75, 76, 77, 78, 79, 80, 81, 84, 86, 87, 89, 91, 93, 97, 102, 104, 108
interview, 29, 35, 36, 100
intimacy, 27
invasive cancer, 24
investment, 7, 22
investment model, 22
isolation, 73, 98, 100
Israel, 95, 97, 98, 100, 105, 107, 109

J

judgment, 68
justice, 86
juvenile justice, 86

K

knee arthroplasty, 56
knowledge acquisition, 52
knowledge construction, 49

L

language, ix, 41, 43, 47, 49, 51, 52, 55, 72, 73
language development, 73
laptop, 54
leadership, 35
learning, 7, 13, 14, 18, 44, 48, 49, 51, 54, 56, 60, 64, 65, 66, 67, 74, 77, 79, 87, 93
leisure, 64
life span, vii
lifestyle, 43
likelihood, 2, 3, 10
limitation, 3, 30, 50
listening, 63
literacy, ix, 47, 48, 49, 50, 52, 53, 54, 55, 56, 57, 58
literature, x, 2, 15, 26, 27, 28, 65, 69, 71, 88, 95, 96, 97, 98, 99, 102, 108
location, viii, 7, 17, 24, 36, 40, 54
logistics, 40
loneliness, 95
longevity, 2
longitudinal studies, 95
longitudinal study, 92, 106, 107
loss of appetite, 99
love, 21
low risk, 5, 7
lying, 75
lymph, 27, 36, 40

lymph node, 27, 36, 40

M

major depression, 106
males, 4, 8, 9, 49, 72, 98, 105, 108
mammography, 10, 19, 20, 25, 44, 58
management, x, 4, 21, 26, 42, 83, 86, 87, 92
marital conflict, 3
marital discord, 5
marital quality, 3, 20, 22
marital status, 30, 36
market, 20
marketing, 7, 8
marriage, 6, 7, 8, 9, 10, 19, 21, 22, 99, 102
married couples, 3, 16, 17
Marx, 105, 108
masculinity, 96
mastectomy, 29, 30, 31, 33, 44
mastery, 63, 99
meals, 100
measurement, 98
measures, viii, ix, 6, 10, 24, 26, 29, 30, 31, 36, 37, 47, 55, 61
media, 48, 71
median, 78
medical care, ix, 36, 47
medication, 10, 99, 101, 104
medication compliance, 10
medicine, 57, 58
men, x, 6, 7, 9, 11, 12, 44, 95, 96, 97, 98, 99, 100, 101, 102, 103, 104, 106, 107, 108
menopause, 25
mental disorder, vii, 80, 91
mental health, x, 12, 28, 30, 37, 41, 83, 84, 85, 86, 87, 88, 89, 90, 91, 92, 93, 94, 107
mental health professionals, 90
mental retardation, 82
mental state, 73, 80
mental states, 73
mentoring, x, 83, 87
messages, 48, 50
meta analysis, 98
meta-analysis, 21
metastatic cancer, 26
Miami, 59
minorities, 48, 92
minority, ix, x, 11, 35, 47, 61, 83, 87
minority groups, 87
miscarriage, x, 95, 96, 97, 99, 102, 103, 105, 108
misconceptions, 9
modeling, 19, 59
models, viii, 13, 17, 18, 24, 56

moderators, 20
money, 8, 9
mood, viii, 24, 26, 27, 28, 29, 31, 38
morbidity, 48
morning, 101
mortality, 25, 48, 98
mortality rate, 25
mothers, 97, 109
motion, 28
motivation, 8, 9, 12, 74, 97
motor behavior, 72
multiculturalism, 84
multi-ethnic, viii, 23, 33, 34
multimedia, 54, 80
multiple factors, 55
multiple regression analysis, 37
multivariate, 19

N

national action, 93
nausea, 30
negative consequences, 4
neuroimaging, 80
neuroscience, 80
neuroticism, 28
New England, 43
New Jersey, 107
New York, 20, 22, 42, 43, 56, 69, 80, 81, 82, 85, 86, 90, 91, 92, 93, 94, 106, 107, 108, 109
nicotine, 57
nodes, 27
noise, 98
nonverbal communication, 72, 73
normal development, vii
nurses, 41
nursing, 41
nurturance, 100
nutrition, 27, 36

O

obligation, 101
observations, 78, 85, 90, 93
optimism, 8, 9, 26
organ, 56
organization, 11, 12
organizations, vii, 51
overweight, 75

P

Pacific, 69
pain, 26, 30, 31, 97, 102, 104
palliative, 37
parental involvement, x, 83
parenting, 97, 103
parents, 8, 9, 20, 21, 58, 62, 73, 74, 75, 87, 88, 96, 97, 100, 107
patient care, 50, 52, 53, 55
peer group, 16, 27
peer support, 27, 28, 29, 44
peers, 59, 72, 77, 78, 87
perception, 8, 12, 64, 101
perceptions, 7, 21, 64, 68, 85, 101
performance, 63
perinatal, 107
perpetration, 4, 13, 14, 15, 19, 22
personal, vii, 3, 9, 15, 32, 60, 63, 74, 99, 108
personal learning, 60
personal relations, 108
personal relationship, 108
personality, vii, 101
personality disorder, vii
persuasion, 105
photographs, 77
physical aggression, 13, 14, 15, 21
physical well-being, viii, 24, 26
Physicians, 44
pilot study, 108
planning, 33, 68, 69
plants, 50
polio, 56
poliovirus, 56
poor, 31, 33, 48, 50, 53, 55, 78, 92
population, ix, 3, 5, 28, 30, 35, 44, 47, 49, 50, 51, 52, 53, 54, 55, 67, 81, 109
positive behaviors, 78, 88
positive feedback, 66
poverty, 90, 93
power, 89
predictors, 11, 13, 17, 20, 21, 28, 31
preference, 8, 9, 65, 73, 104
pregnancy, 96, 109
preschool, 80
preschool children, 80
pressure, 100
prevention, vii, viii, 1, 2, 3, 4, 5, 6, 7, 8, 9, 10, 11, 12, 13, 14, 15, 16, 17, 18, 19, 22, 49, 50, 89, 90, 91, 93
preventive programs, 21
primary school, 81
privacy, 50, 99
problem behavior, x, 3, 17, 71, 75, 76, 77
problem behaviors, 76
problem solving, viii, 3, 15, 23, 41, 87, 96
problem-solving skills, 15
production, 54
professions, 69
profit, 35
program, 3, 4, 5, 6, 7, 8, 9, 10, 13, 14, 15, 17, 18, 19, 20, 21, 22, 29, 43, 57, 59, 60, 62, 65, 66, 67, 85, 87, 89, 90, 91, 92, 108
programming, viii, 2, 3, 4, 5, 7, 8, 9, 10, 11, 12, 13, 14, 15, 16, 17, 18, 42, 91
promote, 81, 89
prostate, 44, 56
prostate cancer, 44, 56
psychiatric morbidity, 44
psychiatrist, 26
psychological distress, 42, 43, 100, 105, 109
psychological well-being, 109
psychologist, 63
psychology, vii, viii, 2, 13, 20, 61, 71, 80
psychopathology, vii, 2, 86, 91, 94
psychosocial stress, 108
psychosocial support, 43
psychotherapy, 19, 63, 69, 92, 108
public health, 58, 89

Q

qualitative research, 64
quality of life, 25, 26, 27, 43, 44
questionnaires, 35, 61

R

race, viii, 24, 28, 37, 39, 41
radiation, 30, 42
radiation therapy, 30
random assignment, viii, 23, 35
range, vii, x, 6, 28, 30, 55, 72, 73, 79, 89, 95
Rapid Case Ascertainment, viii, 23, 29
reading, 58, 77
reading comprehension, 58, 77
realism, 66
reality, 98, 99
recall, 58, 74
reciprocity, 72
recognition, x, 18, 60, 95, 98, 103
recruiting, 8, 16, 17, 60, 61
recurrence, 40, 41
reduction, 12, 26, 27, 49, 54, 99
reflection, 33, 63

Registry, viii, 23, 29, 43
regression, 11, 19
regression equation, 11
rehabilitation, 43, 90
relationship(s), vii, viii, 1, 2, 3, 4, 5, 8, 9, 10, 12, 13, 14, 15, 16, 17, 18, 19, 20, 21, 22, 28, 36, 61, 62, 67, 68, 69, 72, 90, 99, 100, 102, 103, 105, 107, 108, 109
relationship satisfaction, 3
relatives, 40, 96, 101
relevance, 91
reliability, 6, 20
research design, viii, 2
resilience, 88, 93
resolution, 68
resources, ix, 4, 18, 47, 51, 54, 89
responsiveness, 73
restaurants, 35
restructuring, 9
retention, 49
risk, viii, ix, 1, 2, 3, 5, 6, 7, 8, 9, 12, 15, 16, 18, 20, 21, 22, 25, 27, 28, 29, 35, 40, 41, 42, 47, 48, 49, 92, 93, 98, 108
risk factors, 5, 8, 9, 15, 16
RMSEA, 13
role playing, ix, 7, 59, 60, 61, 67
routines, 72, 76, 79
Russia, 100

S

SA, 56
sadness, 97, 98, 99, 101, 102, 104
safety, ix, 35, 47
sample, 4, 5, 11, 13, 14, 17, 29, 31, 35, 36, 72, 79
sampling, 5
satisfaction, 3, 20, 21, 49, 52, 55, 57, 63
savings, 53, 55
SBMH clinics, x, 83, 84, 85, 86, 87, 89
scarcity, 18
scheduling, 40, 62
schizophrenia, vii
school, x, 3, 4, 62, 69, 76, 83, 84, 85, 86, 87, 88, 89, 90, 91, 92, 93, 94
school adjustment, 88
school climate, 88
school performance, 87
scores, 11, 13, 17, 30, 52
SEER Cancer Registry, viii
selecting, 49, 87
self esteem, 96
self-control, 27
self-empowerment, 92

self-esteem, 2, 20, 27, 28, 40
self-image, 26, 28, 30, 31, 36, 39
self-regulation, 21
self-worth, 2
sensitivity, vii, 98, 106
separation, 62, 98, 99, 102, 105, 106, 107, 109
series, ix, 6, 24, 88
severity, 10, 11, 12, 13
sex, 19, 72, 96
sex ratio, 73
sex role, 96
sexuality, 19, 28, 36
sharing, 32, 63, 76, 104
siblings, 100
side effects, 27, 30, 40, 41
sign, 61
similarity, 32, 41
simulation, 59, 70
sites, 35
skills, viii, ix, 3, 4, 7, 20, 23, 24, 26, 34, 41, 45, 48, 51, 53, 56, 59, 60, 61, 62, 63, 67, 68, 69, 73, 75, 76, 77, 78, 79, 80, 81, 87, 88
skills training, ix, 20, 24
smokers, 57
smoking, 36, 49
smoking cessation, 49
social behavior, x, 71, 77, 79, 81
social competence, 81
social environment, ix, 71, 73, 74, 76
social isolation, 98
social life, 102
social norms, 10, 11, 13, 16, 22
social problems, 25, 29, 75, 97
social roles, 39
social situations, 80
social skills, 73, 74, 76, 79
social support, ix, 24, 26, 28, 42, 44, 45, 100, 107
social support network, 100
social withdrawal, 98
social workers, 34, 41
socialization, 73, 96
society, 21, 69, 84, 96, 103
software, 54
SOI, 49
SOI model, 49
somatization, 98, 99, 104
spectrum, 76, 80, 81
speech, 72
spousal bereavement, 98
stability, 3, 20, 21, 22
stabilization, 53
stages, 8, 10
stakeholders, 85

standards, 88
statistical analysis, 42
stereotyping, 4
stigma, 83
stillbirth, 99, 106, 108
strain, 109
strategies, 5, 8, 9, 11, 16, 18, 26, 45, 74, 90, 91
strength, 28, 53, 79, 98, 99
stress, 2, 26, 42, 62, 98
students, x, 13, 20, 60, 61, 62, 63, 67, 68, 75, 78, 80, 83, 85, 88, 90, 100
subgroups, 27, 41
suffering, 96
suicidal ideation, 2
suicide, 95, 99
Sun, 42
supervision, 61, 62, 63, 69, 85
supervisors, 85
supply, ix, 71
survival, 25, 43, 45
survival rate, 25
survivors, 20, 25, 34, 43
susceptibility, 10, 11, 12, 13, 14, 15, 17
Switzerland, 93
sympathy, 96
symptom(s), 30, 37, 38, 39, 63, 72, 98
syndrome, 80
synthesis, 81

time constraints, 55
timing, 27, 28, 29, 42, 68, 98, 99, 101, 102
tissue, 25
trainees, 68
training, ix, 12, 21, 26, 35, 59, 60, 61, 62, 63, 64, 65, 66, 67, 68, 69, 87
trajectory, 2
transcripts, 32, 33, 63, 68
transformation, 44
translation, 51, 52, 53, 57
transmission, 51
transplant recipients, 56
transportation, 31, 33, 35
trial, 35, 44, 51, 52, 57, 101
tumor, 25
tumors, 25

U

unconditional positive regard, 63
undergraduate, ix, 6, 13, 59, 60, 61, 62, 67, 68, 78
undergraduate education, 61
unhappiness, 8, 103
uninsured, 51
United States, 51, 72, 84, 101
universities, 89
urban areas, 84, 88
USSR, 100, 107

T

tactics, 12
tamoxifen, viii, 24, 30
target behavior, 17, 76, 78
target population, 48
teachers, x, 74, 75, 76, 77, 83, 87, 88
teaching, 48, 49, 51, 56, 58, 59, 60, 61, 67, 68, 69, 87
technician, 54
teens, 21
telephone, 36, 53, 101
tension, 36, 64, 65, 99
test-retest reliability, 36
Texas, 88, 90, 93
theory, vii, ix, 10, 18, 19, 20, 21, 47, 48, 49, 56, 63, 71, 73, 74, 79, 80, 109
therapeutic approaches, 2
therapeutic process, 105
therapeutic relationship, 28, 67, 103, 108
therapists, 27, 87, 104, 106
therapy, viii, x, 2, 19, 20, 21, 24, 26, 27, 36, 43, 44, 62, 69, 84, 91, 92, 95, 102, 103, 105, 108
thinking, 74, 99, 104
time commitment, 50

V

vaccine, 57
validation, 3, 42
validity, 55, 65, 79
values, 37, 98
variability, 9, 12, 18, 53
variable(s), viii, 1, 3, 11, 12, 13, 20, 36, 50, 88, 101
variance, 11, 12, 14, 17
variation, 32
variety of domains, 10
victimization, 4, 13, 14, 15, 19
victims, 4, 18, 20, 96
videotape, 56, 57, 58
village, 90
violence, vii, viii, 1, 2, 3, 4, 5, 10, 12, 13, 14, 15, 16, 17, 18, 19, 20, 21, 22, 91
vocabulary, 53
voice, 73, 76
vulnerability, 9

W

weakness, 101
web, 44
well-being, vii, viii, 21, 23, 24, 25, 26, 43, 48, 101
wellness, 41
WHO, 55
Wisconsin, 69
withdrawal, 101
wives, 19, 96, 97, 99, 100, 102, 103
women, viii, ix, x, 6, 7, 8, 9, 10, 11, 12, 17, 19, 21, 22, 23, 24, 25, 26, 27, 28, 29, 30, 31, 32, 33, 34, 35, 36, 37, 38, 39, 40, 41, 42, 43, 44, 56, 95, 96, 97, 98, 99, 100, 101, 104, 105, 106, 107, 108
work environment, 103
workers, 12, 34
workstation, 54
World Health Organization, 48, 88, 93
World Health Organization (WHO), 88
worry, 36, 37, 99
writing, 74, 75

Y

yield, 68, 79
young adults, 5, 9, 16, 19
young women, viii, 23, 25, 29, 33, 42, 43